LARGER

DATE DUE

~~OC 25 05~~			

PE   N

LANGUAGE & CULTURE CENTER
UNIVERSITY OF HOUSTON

Prentice Hall Regents
Englewood Cliffs, NJ 07632

...ss Cataloging-in-Publication Data

...nited States / by Penny

1. Tales—Unites States.   2. Heroes —United States—Biography.
3. United States—History—Biography.   4. Frontier and pioneer life—
United States.   I. Title
GR105.5.C36   1994
398.2'0973—dc20   93-47027
                                                               CIP

Acquisitions Editor: Nancy Baxer
Director of Production and Manufacturing: David Riccardi
Editorial Production/Design Manager: Dominick Mosco
Electronic/production supervision, interior design, and electronic art: Ken Liao
Production Coordinator: Ray Keating
Cover Coordinator: Merle Krumper

Illustrator: Frank Cyrsky
Cover Designer: Tom Nery

© 1994 by Prentice Hall Regents
Prentice-Hall, Inc.
A Paramount Communications Company
Englewood Cliffs, New Jersey 07632

Printed in the United States of America

10   9   8   7   6   5   4   3

ISBN 0-13-299470-4

Prentice-Hall International (UK) Limited, London
Prentice-Hall of Australia Pty. Limited, Sydney
Prentice-Hall Canada Inc., Toronto
Prentice-Hall Hispanoamericana, S.A., Mexico
Prentice-Hall of India Private Limited, New Delhi
Prentice-Hall of Japan, Inc., Tokyo
Simon & Schuster Asia Pte. Ltd., Singapore
Editora Prentice-Hall do Brasil, Ltda., Rio de Janeiro

LARGER THAN LIFE:
FOLK HEROES OF THE UNITED STATES

LARGER THAN LIFE:
FOLK HEROES OF THE UNITED STATES

INTRODUCTION

The tales and poetry in this book are traditional, which means that they belong to the people of the United States. My aim is to allow secondary and adult students who are learning English at the high-beginner to low-intermediate level to read the stories in simple language and to relate to the poetry. When I first came to the United States, I sometimes heard people talking about stories which meant nothing to me but which clearly conveyed a lot to the other people in the conversation. Now when people talk about George Washington and the cherry tree, I know it's a metaphor for honesty—one more hold upon the culture, one less thing to have explained . . .

When I began my selection for this book, I looked for personalities and stories which many people born and raised in the United States were likely to know. I did my research in the library, the supermarket, the cafeteria, and the gymnasium. A few of these stories and verses will be familiar to many Americans, and most will at least be recognized. I suspect that their themes are already deep in the American consciousness, for many of the pieces have a breadth and a sense of space which seems to me to be essentially American.

Some of these stories are about people who can be traced as historical figures, although the particular stories in this book may not be verifiable. Thus, we have wily Davy Crockett tricking a storekeeper and coming back to confess later; and we have the heroic John Henry breaking his great heart in an unwinnable contest with a machine. One is a figure of history, the other of legend—yet both live on and contribute to the culture of the United States.

Wherever possible I have used contemporary illustrations which I feel add dignity and authenticity to the book. The vocabulary is heavily contextualized so that the students may learn to deduce meaning. I looked for verse which would not intimidate the high-beginner to low-intermediate reader with its obscurity.

The exercises take the students *into, through,* and *beyond* the story, and are more fully discussed in the Teacher's Guide. I have tried to provide opportunities for cooperative learning, and to offer enough variety to cater for the needs of different students.

The students are required to read the story at least twice: first to get the general meaning, and later to seek for detail. The Teacher's Guide includes additional notes for the teacher, an answer key, and a prepared quiz and dictation after each story which may be photocopied for the class.

My references are cited in the Teacher's Guide in the chapters where they were especially relevant. I would like to acknowledge the global influence of Roger E. W-B Olsen's wisdom and counsel, expressed in his editing and review of this manuscript, and Pat Rigg's article "Whole Language in TESOL" in the *TESOL Quarterly,* Volume 25, Number 3.

I hope that you all enjoy using these stories and verses as much as I have enjoyed collecting them.

Penny Cameron

LARGER THAN LIFE:
FOLK HEROES OF THE UNITED STATES

1

JOHN HENRY

We don't know who the real John Henry was, but we do know his story. After the Civil War, people wanted to move easily across the United States. They needed trains in order to travel, and the trains needed tunnels through the mountains. John Henry was one of the men who built tunnels for the trains.

Look very carefully at the picture on the next page. A long time ago, in 1870, people wanted to build a tunnel through a mountain. This was the way they used to put dynamite into the rock to blow it up.

The man holding the bar was called a shaker. The man with the hammer was the steel-driving man. Together they dug a hole in the rock for the explosives. Later, other people put dynamite into the hole and blew up the rock. When you are reading the story, think about the hard work these people were doing.

JOHN HENRY AND THE STEAM DRILL

BEFORE THE STORY

Talk to your classmates. Be ready to tell your teacher what other people in your group said.

1. Look at the picture on page 2. Then answer these questions.

    a. What are the people doing?

    b. Describe the man with the hammer.

    c. How heavy do you think the hammer is? Underline the answer.
    (1 pound = 0.45 kg)

          2 pounds   12 pounds   40 pounds   60 pounds

    d. Is it dangerous for the man holding the drill in place? Why?

    e. How do you think the steel driver and the shaker who holds the drill feel about their jobs?

2. What do these words mean?

    hole   dynamite   gunpowder   explosive   dust

    tunnel   steel driver   shaker   drill   hammer

3. This story is about a race between a man and a machine. Do you think the man will win? Why? Write down your group's prediction about whether John Henry or the machine will win.

    _____

    _____

    _____

4. Show your teacher what these words and phrases mean:

    tired   sick   pray   hiss   crackle   bury

    worried   ahead   cheer   rush   nervous

5. **Now read the story once, or listen while your teacher reads. Don't worry if you don't understand all the words when you first read a story. Just try to get the main idea.**

JOHN HENRY AND THE STEEL DRILL

This story happened a long time ago, in 1870.

John Henry was a very strong man. He was tall and powerful. John Henry was a steel driver. In fact, he was the best steel driver in America.

5   It was John Henry's job to drive a steel drill into rock. He had another man to help him. That man was called a shaker. It was his job to turn the drill in the rock and shake it a little. That made the rock dust fall out of the hole. Then the steel-driving man would hit the drill again.

10   So John Henry hit the steel drill. Then the shaker turned the drill. Then John Henry hit the drill again. And the shaker turned it again. And John Henry hit it . . .

When the hole was deep enough, other men put gunpowder into the hole in the rock. Then they blew it up, and the rock broke

15 into hundreds of little pieces.

That's the way they built the tunnels for the railroads. It was hard, dangerous work, and the most important person was the steel driver. If he drove a lot of holes in a short time, the work was quick. But if he was slow, everyone had to wait, because there were no holes

20 for the gunpowder.

Most people worked slowly, but John Henry never did. Perhaps he never got tired. He worked from morning to night, swinging his hammer. The other men stopped, but John Henry went on and on.

Most men used a six-pound hammer, but John Henry used a

25 hammer that weighed twelve pounds. He swung it from his shoulder. The hammer came down fast and hard, and it drove the drill into the rock.

In the year 1870, John Henry was working on the Chesapeake and Ohio Railroad. The railroad workers were making a tunnel

30 through the Big Bend Mountain in West Virginia.

The rock was hard and the work took a long time. Sometimes the men sang as they worked. Their big hammers rose and fell. They sang, and they hit the steel drill in time with their song.

And so they worked for more than two years. It was not easy to

35 make that tunnel! The men were tired. Only John Henry worked as hard as ever.

One day a stranger came to see the captain of the steel-driving gang.

"I have something to show you," the stranger said. "I have a
40 machine that drives steel."

John Henry's captain laughed. "I have the best steel-driving man in the United States right here," he said. "I have John Henry. He never stops working."

"My machine doesn't eat," the stranger pointed out. "It never
45 gets tired and it never gets sick."

"Neither does John Henry," the captain said. "He's never sick, and he just works on and on without getting tired. Anything your machine can do, John Henry can do better."

"I don't believe you," the stranger said.

50 "All right," John Henry's captain said. "We'll have a race, John Henry against the steam drill. If your machine wins, I buy it. If John Henry wins, you pay him $100, and you give me the steam drill. But I warn you, you'll lose."

"Oh, I don't think so," the stranger said.

How do you think John Henry will feel about the race?
Do you think the other people who work in the tunnel are nervous?
What will happen to them if the machine wins?

55 People came from miles around to see the race.

John Henry was getting ready for the race. He chose a twenty-pound hammer. Then he talked with his shaker. "I'll swing very hard," he said. "Pray I don't hit you. If I do, you'll die, and they'll bury you in the ground."

60 The shaker smiled at John Henry. "You're the best steel-driving man in the world," he said. "I'm safe with you. I'm not afraid. Go out and beat the machine, John Henry! Show them all that people are better than machines."

"I'll beat that machine," John Henry said, "or I'll die with my
65 hammer in my hand."

A crowd gathered. Everyone looked at the machine. It seemed very big. Men were putting fuel in the firebox. When the water got hot, it made steam and drove the engine.

At last, everything was ready. The crowd was quiet. Some of the
70 people in the crowd were nervous.

"What will happen to us if the machine works faster than John Henry?" one man asked his friend. "Will the railroad company buy machines? Will there be any jobs for us?"

All the steel drivers were worried. They looked at John Henry,
75 and they saw how strong he looked. They felt better. "Good luck!" they called out.

One man said to another, "John Henry isn't just strong, he's got courage."

"You mean that he's brave?" the other man asked.

80 "Courage is being brave, but it's also being able to go on when things are difficult. John Henry's like that. He won't give up."

John Henry smiled, and waited. Everyone was very quiet. Then the captain of the steel-driving gang fired a gun into the air, and the race started.

85 The machine hissed and crackled, and it hit the steel into the rock. John Henry swung his hammer hard, and he sang as he swung. He worked hard, but so did the steam drill. It never paused, but just went on and on.

John Henry said to his shaker, "How am I doing?"

90 The shaker looked worried. "The machine is ahead of you!" he said.

John Henry worked harder. He was catching up.

The machine just went on and on. All the men looked at it. They worried about their jobs. The machine was not getting tired,
95 but even John Henry had to rest sometime . . .

There was a roar and a whoosh! and the machine was quiet.

The men cheered. "It's broken!" the shaker said.

"Good!" John Henry said. "Now I can get ahead!" He raised his hammer again.

100 The man who owned the machine hurried to fix it. John Henry kept on hammering. The machine was quiet. The men felt happy, listening to John Henry's hammer hitting the drill. It was a familiar sound, and it made them feel comfortable.

The machine started up again.

105 The hours passed. John Henry wasn't singing anymore. The people in the crowd watched anxiously. All anyone heard was the hiss and thud of the machine, and the crash of John Henry's hammer.

110 The race was nearly over. "Keep going!" the shaker said. "Just keep going. The race will be over at half past two."

John Henry nodded. He had no breath left to speak. His hammer rose and fell, rose and fell . . . At last it was half past two. The race was over.

115 The captain measured all the drill holes. He checked to see how deep they were, and he added them all up.

"John Henry, you drove fourteen feet!" the captain said. "The machine only drove nine! You win, John Henry! You win!"

Everyone cheered and yelled, and rushed to John Henry. But the big man was falling. His friends helped him to lie down on the 120 ground. He was very heavy, and it was difficult to lower him gently.

The machine hissed and stopped. Now the whole world was very quiet. Everyone gathered around John Henry, and they listened as he spoke. "I'm dying," he said softly. "I broke myself with hammering."

125 The people were silent. Then John Henry, the best steel-driving man in the world, died. But his story lives on, and when we think of John Henry, we think of strength and courage.

AFTER THE STORY

A. Work with a classmate, and answer this question.

Who won the race? Underline the correct answer.

John Henry   the steam drill   the captain

B. Read the story again. Look at the picture. Work with a classmate, and try to guess the meaning of the words you don't know. If you can't guess, you may look in the dictionary.

C. Now answer these questions.

1. Say whether these statements are true or false. Check under *True* or *False*. If they are false, write the correct answer below. We did the first one for you.

	True	False
1. John Henry was a weak man. *John Henry was a very strong man.*		✔
2. Driving steel was easy work.		
3. The machine worked hard and never stopped.		
4. John Henry's shaker helped him.		
5. The other steel drivers did not want John Henry to win.		

2. Match the speakers with what they are saying. We did the first one for you.

1. John Henry

2. The man who owned the steam drill

3. John Henry's captain

4. John Henry's shaker

a. You're the best steel-driving man in the world. I'm safe with you.

b. I'll die with my hammer in my hand.

c. I have a machine that drives steel.

d. I have the best steel-driving man in the United States right here.

D. Now study some words.

1. Look at these words, and underline the word in each row which has a different meaning. We did the first one for you.

   1. strong   powerful   <u>dangerous</u>
   2. quick   slow   fast
   3. crowd   people   captain
   4. safe   worried   nervous
   5. silent   hot   quiet
   6. cheer   break   yell

2. Look at these different ways we can use the word *hard*. Match these words with the way *hard* is used in each sentence. We did the first one for you.

   1. John Henry worked <u>hard</u>.   a. difficult
   2. The hammer came down   b. difficult to break
      fast and <u>hard</u>.
   3. The rock was <u>hard</u>.   c. heavily
   4. It was <u>hard</u>, dangerous work.   d. well, and with a lot
                                               of effort

E. Think about the story.

1. Make a list of the words in the story which describe John Henry. Work with a classmate.

2. With a classmate, look back through the story to help you see John Henry more clearly. Talk with your classmate, and write a paragraph about John Henry.

   OR

3. How does this story make you feel about John Henry? Would you like to meet him? Write your answer on the next page, and explain why you would (or would not) like to meet John Henry.

_____

_____

_____

_____

_____

F. Talk about these things with your classmates.

- What jobs do you know that machines can do? Make a list on the chalkboard.
- Did people do these jobs before? What happened to the people?

BEYOND THE STORY

G. Now do these activities.

1. Go to the library and find out about railroads and railroad tunnels. Share what you learn with your teacher and classmates.

2. Now answer this question. Write your answer in a few sentences.

   What do you think the United States was like before there were railroads?

   _____

   _____

   _____

   _____

   _____

3. Three students can pretend to be John Henry's boss, the shaker, and a member of the crowd. You are there at the end of the race. What happens next? What do people say and do? Prepare a role-play.

4. Do another role-play: Interview the man who owned the machine and John Henry's captain. Work with your partner to decide what questions you will ask. Get your teacher to choose two students to pretend to be the machine owner and John Henry's captain. Then write an account of what they say for a newspaper called *The Railroad Gazette*.

Ballad: John Henry

Now that you know his story, read this poem about John Henry. Then say the poem aloud. When you say the poem, be sure to listen for the rhythm, and stress the important words. Listen for the rhythm of the hammer.

John Henry

John Henry says to his captain
"A man is nothing but a man
And before I'll let that steam drill beat me down
I'll die with my hammer in my hand, Oh Lord,
I'll die with my hammer in my hand."

John Henry says to his shaker,
"Shaker, you'd better pray
For if ever I miss that piece of steel,
Tomorrow'll be your burial day,
Tomorrow'll be your burial day."

John Henry hammering on the mountain,
As the whistle blows for half past two.
The last words the captain hears him say
"I just hammered my insides in two,
Lord, I hammered my insides in two."

They carried him down by the river
And buried him in the sand,
And everybody that passed that way
Said, "There lies that steel-driving man
There lies that steel-driving man."

H. Answer these questions about the poem.

1. Do you think you could set this poem to music? What sort of musical instrument would you use?

2. What is your favorite line in the poem? Why do you like it?

3. Do you think the poem helps people remember John Henry? Why? What else makes people remember the story?

2

GEORGE WASHINGTON
1732–1799

George Washington was certainly a real person, but we cannot be so sure about the story of George Washington and the cherry tree. It is a story which people tell to show why George Washington was so honest. People always felt they could trust him, because he always told the truth.

Washington was born in Virginia, and he fought against the French between 1755 and 1759. He fought against the British and led the Continental Army from July of 1775. In 1781 Washington defeated the British at Yorktown and the war ended.

Washington became the first President of the United States in 1789. He was President for the next eight years and he retired in 1797.

The caption, which you can barely see on this picture, says
"Father, I can not tell a lie: I cut the tree."

GEORGE WASHINGTON AND THE CHERRY TREE

BEFORE THE STORY

Talk to your classmates. Be ready to tell your teacher what other people in your group said.

1. Look at the picture on page 14. Then answer these questions.

   a. What do you and the people in your group see? Describe the picture.

   b. What does the picture tell you about the man and the boy?

   c. Find the bark of the tree and its branches. What has happened to its trunk? What is lying under the tree?

   d. Look at their clothes. What year do you think this picture shows? Underline your answer.

      1738   1838   1938

      Now look at page 13 and check your answer. How do you know you are right?

   e. What do you know about George Washington? How can you find out more?

   f. What does "tell the truth" mean? What does "tell a lie" mean?

2. Show the teacher what these words mean

      angry   furious   sick   afraid   beat (somebody)   chop (wood)

3. Ask the others in your group if they have ever used an ax. What happened? How did they feel?

4. Read the beginning of the story (page 16, lines 1–11), down to "You'll beat me, or send me to bed without my dinner." What do you think is going to happen in this story? Make notes of your prediction. Your prediction is what your group thinks will happen.

5. **Now read the story once, or listen while your teacher reads. Don't worry if you don't understand all the words when you first read a story. Just try to get the main idea.**

GEORGE WASHINGTON AND THE CHERRY TREE

George Washington's father loved the truth. He hated lies and he hated people who told lies. He loved honesty and telling the truth.

"You must always tell the truth," he told his young son. "Always
5   say what is true. If you lie, I will be very angry."

George was five years old. He listened carefully to his father. He had one big question.

"But Father," George replied, "what if you are really angry? What if I do something wrong, and you beat me? If I tell a lie, you
10   won't know I was bad. But if I tell you, you will know. Then you will punish me. You'll beat me, or send me to bed without my dinner."

"George," his father said, "I will not hurt you. I will never punish you if you tell the truth."

A year passed. George Washington was growing up. He
15   remembered his father's words: "Tell the truth. I will not punish you."

Old Mr. Washington had a cherry tree in his garden. It was a beautiful tree, but it was not strong. It was an English tree, so it did not grow easily in Virginia. Mr. Washington loved it, and he often came to look at it.

20   When George was six, somebody gave him a hatchet. A hatchet is a small ax with a short handle. You can use it for cutting wood.

George loved his hatchet. He went around his father's house looking for things to chop. Then he went into the garden. He chopped up an old piece of wood. He cut up a wooden box.

25   George came to the cherry tree. He tried to cut a little bit of the bark on its trunk. George swung his hatchet. He made a beautiful clean cut. The cherry wood was good to cut, not too soft and not too hard. George cut it again.

What do you think will happen?
What will George's father say or do?

George was only six. He forgot about his father. He just kept
30   chopping. Soon there were big cuts on the trunk of the tree. George went inside.

Some days passed, and Mr. Washington was walking around his
35   garden. When he came to visit his tree, he was most surprised. The
tree looked very sick. It was losing its leaves, and its branches hung
down very heavily.

"Whatever is wrong?" he said. He looked at the trunk of the
tree. There were deep cuts in the wood. They were exactly the size of
40   the blade of George's ax. Mr. Washington was furious.

"George!" he cried angrily. "Come here!"

George Washington came to his father.

"George," Mr. Washington said, "look at my tree. This is the tree
I like the best. And somebody has hurt it. Somebody has cut into its
45   wood." He paused, and then he looked at his son.

George was afraid. His father was very angry. But then he
remembered what Mr. Washington said.

George drew a deep breath. "I cannot tell a lie," he said. "I cut
the tree, Father."

50   Mr. Washington's face went very red. He looked very angry—
and very frightening. George backed away.

Look at the prediction you made at the beginning of the story.
Do you still expect your prediction to be right?

Then Mr. Washington held his arms out. "You're a good boy,
George," he said. "You always tell the truth. I am sad about the tree,
but I am very happy that my son is so honest. You will grow into an
55   honest man."

AFTER THE STORY

A. Work with a classmate, and answer this question.

Who made cuts in the cherry tree? Underline the correct answer.

George Washington   George Washington's father

some other person

B. Read the story again. Look at the picture. Work with a classmate, and try
to guess the meaning of the words you don't know. If you can't guess,
you may look in the dictionary.

C. Now answer these questions. Put a circle around the letter which is the best answer. We did the first one for you.

1. Why was Mr. Washington pleased with George?
   a. Because George hurt the tree.
   (b.) Because George told the truth.
   c. Because Mr. Washington did not want the tree.

2. Why was George afraid to tell his father?
   a. He knew that Mr. Washington loved the tree.
   b. He was afraid of his father at all times.
   c. He knew that his father was very angry.
   d. Both *a.* and *c.*

3. Why do you think people tell this story?
   a. To show how George Washington came to be so honest.
   b. To stop children from chopping trees.
   c. To show that Mr. Washington was not a good father.
   d. Both *a.* and *b.*

D. Match the words with their meanings. We did the first one for you.

1. punish		a.	telling the truth
2. angry		b.	the outer covering of a tree
3. hatchet		c.	the part of a tree where leaves grow
4. true		d.	very annoyed, but not furious
5. bark		e.	not false
6. branch		f.	a small ax
7. honesty		g.	to make somebody suffer for doing something wrong

E. Think about the story.

1. How does this story make you feel about George Washington? Look back through the story with a classmate. Talk with your classmate and write your answers below.

    _____

    _____

    _____

    _____

    _____

2. Why do you think people keep telling this story? Do you think it is true? Talk with your classmate and write your answers below.

    _____

    _____

    _____

    _____

F. Talk about the story.

1. Do you know any other stories about people being honest when it was dangerous to tell the truth? Tell the class. These notes may help you.
    *   Tell where the story happened, and when.
    *   Tell who the people in the story are.
    *   Tell what happened first, second, and third.
    *   Tell what the result or conclusion of the story is.

    OR

    *   Tell a personal story about lying or telling the truth. Use the same notes to help you.

    _____

    _____

    _____

    _____

    _____

2. What influence do you think a parent has on a child? Can parents teach children to be honest or to lie? Talk with your classmates, and ask them to fill out the grid below. If they believe a statement is absolutely true, they will mark 5. Ask your classmates to explain their answers.

	Completely false			Absolutely true	
	1	2	3	4	5
Only parents can teach children to be honest.					
Children will learn more about honesty from their teachers than from their parents.					
A dishonest child comes from bad parents.					
Cruel parents make children lie.					

BEYOND THE STORY

G. Now do these activities.

1. Go to the library and find out more about George Washington. Share what you learn with your teacher and classmates.

2. Change the story: George Washington's father punished him severely. What did George say and think? Make a role-play.

3. Is it ever right to tell a lie? Work with a partner and try to think of a time when it is better to tell a lie.

4. Now answer this question. Why could people believe this story about George Washington and the cherry tree?

SONG: YANKEE DOODLE

George Washington led the Revolutionary War against the British. The American soldiers did not have fancy uniforms, and the British laughed at them. The British made up a song called "Yankee Doodle." In it they talked about a Yankee (American) dandy. A dandy is someone who dresses very fashionably.

The Americans took the song for themselves after they won the battle against the British at Yorktown.

YANKEE DOODLE

Yankee Doodle went to town
A-riding on a pony
He stuck a feather in his cap
And called it macaroni!

Yankee Doodle went to town
He bought a bag of peaches,
He rode so fast a-coming back,
He smashed them all to pieces.

Yankee Doodle, find a girl,
Yankee Doodle dandy,
Take her to the fair today
And buy a box of candy!

Yankee Doodle keep it up,
Yankee Doodle dandy!
Mind the music and the steps,
And with the girls be handy!

H. Think about the song.

1. A pony is a small horse that children ride. Why do you think the British said "riding on a pony," not "riding on a horse"?

2. Irony is when you say one thing but mean another. For instance, it is an irony to call someone in ragged clothes a dandy. Find words in the song which have been used so that they will sound silly or ironic.

3. Why do you think the Americans took the song?

4. Does this song make you want to do any of these things?

      dance   march   run   sleep

Why?

5. Work with your group to illustrate this song. You can do it like a comic strip or you can do one picture. Stick figures are fine! Be ready to explain your picture to the rest of the class.

3

JOHNNY APPLESEED
JOHN CHAPMAN
1774–1845

Johnny Appleseed's real name was John Chapman. He brought apple seeds to Ohio and Indiana, and he left behind many stories. These stories all tell about a shy, gentle, religious man. He treated everyone kindly, and although people laughed at him, they loved him too.

The people in Ohio and Indiana had hard lives in the early part of the nineteenth century. They were often called settlers, because they had gone to settle on land which nobody had farmed before. The farms were a long way apart from each other, and people were very lonely. Often the family—mother, father, and children—saw nobody else for weeks at a time. There were no real roads and it was hard for the farmers to get things to town to sell. Often the food they wanted to sell went bad on the way to the town.

Johnny planted his apple seeds in good places near the rivers. Then he went away, and the apple trees grew. The next year that he came back he gave the young trees to the farmers. He kept moving all the time, planting seeds.

The settlers were very happy to take the apple trees. Apples do not go bad easily. You can make a lot of good things to eat with apples. It is no wonder that people loved Johnny Appleseed.

JOHNNY APPLESEED

Johnny Appleseed, A Gentle Man

Before the Story

Talk to your classmates. Be ready to tell your teacher what the other people in your group said.

1. Now answer this question. What is the difference between a gentleman and a gentle man?

2. Look at the picture on page 24. Now answer these questions.

   a. What do you and the other people in your group see? Work together to describe the man in the picture.

   b. Do you think the man is rich or poor? Why?

   c. Look at his feet. What is he wearing on them?

   d. What sort of tree is in the picture?

   e. What is at the man's waist?

3. Skim page 23 and find out when Johnny Appleseed was born. What was his real name?

4. Find Ohio and Indiana on the map below. The United States looked like this in 1800. Have you ever been in a very lonely place? What do you think Ohio and Indiana were like in 1800?

5. Work with your group, and make a list of things that we have now that did not exist in 1800.

6. Answer these questions.

   a. Do you know what a settler was? Scan page 23 to find out.

   b. How did people travel before there were roads?

   c. How do you think they took their crops to market?

7. Show the teacher what these words mean.

   shy   angry   hungry   paddle   hurt   slap   smelly

8. What do you know about apple trees? Write the words you think of on the diagram below.

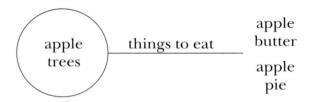

9. **Now read the story once, or listen while your teacher reads. Don't worry if you don't understand all the words when you first read a story. Just try to get the main idea.**

Johnny Appleseed, A Gentle Man

Johnny Appleseed's real name was John Chapman. He got the name "Appleseed" because he went around Ohio and Indiana planting apple seeds. The apple seeds grew into apple trees, and Johnny Appleseed gave the young trees to the
5   farmers. Apple orchards remind us of Johnny Appleseed.

Johnny Appleseed was an eccentric; he did things differently from other people. He certainly did not look like other people. He wore ragged clothes. He had holes in his trousers and his shirt. His hair was long and messy. He traveled barefoot and alone through
10   dangerous territory.

There is a story that during one freezing November, a kind farmer gave Johnny Appleseed a pair of shoes. A few days later, the farmer met Johnny Appleseed again. His feet were bare and half frozen. The farmer was angry, but Johnny Appleseed told him the
15   following story.

Johnny Appleseed had met a cold, hungry family. They were going westward, but they had no shoes. So Johnny Appleseed gave them the farmer's shoes. The family asked if he wanted to travel with them, but Johnny said no. He was a shy man. He did not want to be
20   with other people, especially strangers.

Johnny Appleseed walked a long way by himself. Sometimes he brought a horse with him to carry the seeds. Sometimes he traveled on the rivers. Once, he tied two canoes together, and he paddled his load of apple seeds for a long way up the Ohio River. But usually he
25   walked, and a long, slow journey it was.

Johnny Appleseed knew what a good crop apples were. There were no roads, so people rode horses or walked. It was difficult to take food from the farm to the market in town. Sometimes the farmers walked and led a horse or mule with produce on its back.
30   Sometimes they used canoes to paddle their crop down the rivers. But it was very difficult, and often corn spoiled between the farm and the market. Apples don't rot as easily as corn. The farmers could take apples to the market. Even if the trip was long and slow, the apples stayed fresh for a long time. So apples were a very important
35   crop for the early settlers.

If they kept the apples on the farm, the farm people could use them for a long time. They could dry them and eat them in winter. They could make apple butter or apple cider. The apple was a very useful fruit.

40 Johnny Appleseed passed through difficult, dangerous country to take his apple seeds to the farms. There were wild animals and poisonous snakes, but Johnny Appleseed was not afraid. Ordinary people wore heavy shoes and put padding around their pant legs to protect them from snakes. Johnny Appleseed marched on, barefoot.

The next part of the story is about Johnny Appleseed and animals.
1. *How do you think he will treat animals?*
2. *Will he be kind to animals?*
3. *What if the animal hurts him?*
4. *Is an insect an animal?*
5. *What is a hornet? Can it hurt you?*

45 Johnny Appleseed loved all animals. One night, when he was sleeping outdoors, he noticed that the mosquitoes were coming to the light of his fire. He watched, and he saw the insects burn themselves. He quickly put out the fire, because he did not want to kill another living creature.

50 Another night Johnny Appleseed was sleeping in a very large hollow log. He lit a fire just outside, and then he heard something moving at the other end of the log. It was a mother bear and her cub! Quickly, Johnny put out the fire and slept on the snow in the open instead.

55 Once a rattlesnake bit Johnny Appleseed. Before he had time to think about what he was doing, he killed it. Poor Johnny Appleseed felt very bad about what he had done. "Poor fellow," he said. "He did not mean to hurt me."

One day Johnny Appleseed was helping some settlers to build a
60 road. One of the men bumped a hornets' nest, and the angry insects chased the people. One of the hornets flew inside Johnny's clothes and stung him. The other men slapped at the insects to kill them, but Johnny Appleseed removed the hornet very gently. Once again, he said that the creature did not mean to hurt him. He was careful
65 not to hurt the hornet.

Other people laughed at him, but they laughed in a kind way.

They knew that Johnny Appleseed was kind to their children, and he did not ever want to hurt anybody. All he wanted to do was to plant apple seeds.

70   The settlers did have one reason to be angry with Johnny Appleseed. He planted dog fennel wherever he went. The settlers thought it was smelly and of no use. Johnny Appleseed thought it helped to cure a disease called malaria. Unfortunately, the settlers were right, and Johnny Appleseed was wrong: dog fennel is a

75 nuisance, and it does not make people with malaria get well again. It was not a good idea to plant it. But people loved Johnny Appleseed so much that they forgot about the dog fennel. They remember him for the apple trees.

    Johnny Appleseed died in 1845, and people remember him

80 kindly today as the man who brought apples to the settlers of the West.

AFTER THE STORY

A. Work with a classmate and answer this question. Underline the correct answer.

What made Johnny Appleseed different?
    his clothes   what he did

    the way he looked   all these things

B. **Read the story again**. Look at the picture. Work with a classmate, and try to guess the meaning of the words you don't know. If you can't guess, you may look in the dictionary.

C. Now answer these questions.

1. Underline the correct word in the parentheses. We did the first one for you.

    Johnny Appleseed took (1. *orange* *apple* *peach*) seeds and grew apple trees for the early settlers around Ohio. He usually (2. *walked* *rode* *drove*). The roads were (3. *excellent* *not real roads at all* *straight and wide*).

Johnny Appleseed was always (4. *cruel   mean   kind*) to animals. He felt very sad when he killed a (5. *rattlesnake   bear   hornet*) after it bit him.

Johnny Appleseed made one big mistake: he thought that dog fennel could (6. *cure   make worse   prevent*) the disease malaria. This was not true.

2. Quickly find the paragraphs in the chapter that explain why apples were a good crop for the early settlers. (When you look quickly for special information like this, it is called scanning.) Write the line number where the paragraphs begin and end:
Line _____ to line _____.

D. Put a circle around the letter of the correct definition. We did the first one for you.

1. An eccentric is somebody who
   a. does things differently from other people.
   b. lives alone.
   c. reads books.

2. Ragged clothes are
   a. clean, new clothes.
   b. old clothes with holes in them.
   c. fashionable clothes.

3. When you are barefoot, you
   a. have new shoes.
   b. have old shoes.
   c. have no shoes.

4. A crop is
   a. food a farmer grows.
   b. any food.
   c. dried food.

5. A creature is

   a. any animal or insect.

   b. any plant, animal, or insect.

   c. any plant.

6. A nuisance is

   a. something everybody likes.

   b. something nobody wants.

   c. a new idea.

E. Work with a classmate. Look back through the story, and write a description of Johnny Appleseed, below.

_____

_____

_____

_____

_____

F. Work with your classmates. Find examples in the story which show that Johnny Appleseed was kind. Put them on the chalkboard.

_____

_____

_____

_____

_____

BEYOND THE STORY

G. Now do these activities.

1. Tell a story about someone you know who did something kind. Explain who the person was, what he or she did, and why it was kind. What were the results of the kind action?

2. Do you know any eccentric people? Work with your classmates, and make up a story about a strange person. You may act out the story if you wish.

3. Pretend you are a farmer who knew Johnny Appleseed and talk about meeting him. What did your family think of him? Was he good to your children?

4. Pretend you are a hunter and tell another hunter about the way Johnny Appleseed treats animals. Make a role-play or tell a story.

5. Go to the library and find out more about Johnny Appleseed. Share what you learn with your teacher and classmates.

4

PAUL BUNYAN

Paul Bunyan was a very strong and very large man. He lived in America during the nineteenth century.

People say that Paul Bunyan came from Canada. He was a logger, somebody who cuts down trees. They say that he could carry 500 pounds over rough ground. This was very important. People who worked as loggers had to be very strong. It was hard, heavy work.

Some people say that Paul Bunyan fought against the troops of the English Queen, Victoria, in 1837. Then he came to work in America.

"Paul Bunyan and the Winter of the Blue Snow" tells how Paul Bunyan found Babe, the Blue Ox. You will find that the whole story is larger than life.

PAUL BUNYAN AND
THE WINTER OF THE BLUE SNOW

BEFORE THE STORY

Talk to your classmates. Be ready to tell your teacher what other people in your group said.

1. Look at the picture on page 34. Then answer these questions. Describe the man. What size is he? How do you know?

2. Look back at page 33. Then answer these questions.

   a. How many pounds (1 lb = 0.45 kg) could Paul Bunyan carry? _____
   Why was that important?

   b. Can you think of an object that weighs 100 lbs? 500 lbs?

   c. Look in an elevator, and see how much weight and how many people it can carry. Share you information with the class. Can all elevators carry the same weight/number of people? Is there a formula?

3. Do you know what snow looks like? What color is it? What other words do you think of when you think of snow? Look at this word diagram about snow.

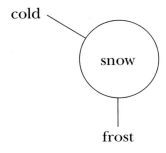

4. These are all exaggerations:
   - I saw a cat as big as a lion.
   - He grew a flower as tall as a tree.
   - She has a dog as heavy as a horse.

They all say that something is bigger, or taller, or heavier, or in some way *more* than it really is. An exaggeration is not true. There are a lot of exaggerations in this story about Paul Bunyan.

5. Show the teacher what these words mean:

    cold   gentle   softly   still   stiff   weak

6. Circle the words and phrases which are about being very big.

    huge   little   baby   big enough to hold a city

    giant   easy   enormous

7. Try to answer these questions. What is an ox calf? What does *newborn* mean?

8. This story is about a huge man and an enormous blue ox. Do you think you will believe everything in this story? Do you think that blue snow is magical? Will strange things happen? Talk to your classmates, and write here your group's predictions of what will happen.

    _____

    _____

    _____

    _____

    _____

9. **Now read the story once, or listen while your teacher reads. Don't worry if you don't understand all the words when you first read a story. Just try to get the main idea.**

Paul Bunyan and
the Winter of the Blue Snow

It was wintertime. The snow was falling gently. The snowflakes were big, and blue, and very cold; this was the winter of the blue snow.

The snow fell for hours. At first it fell softly and lay gently on the
5 ground. But then a wind blew, and the snow fell quickly. It grew colder and colder. The blue snow lay deep and thick, like a carpet on the ground.

All night the blue snow fell. In the morning the whole world was blue.

10 Paul Bunyan looked out of his cave. He saw the blue snow. He was very surprised. "I'll see what my books say," he thought.

Paul Bunyan went back into the cave where he lived and looked around him. His home was huge. The cave was big enough to hold a city.

15 When Paul studied, he wrote on the cave floor with a pine tree. Oh, it wasn't an enormous pine tree. It was a little pine tree. Paul trimmed all its branches to make it easy to hold. How big was it? Well, perhaps it was just seven feet high. That was a nice size for a pencil for Paul Bunyan.

20 Paul picked up his pine tree pencil. But he didn't want to study anymore.

Paul took another pine tree. This tree still had some branches. He combed his beard with it.

"I think I'll go out and look at the snow," Paul said. So he put on
25 his huge coat and went outside.

The whole world looked beautiful. Everything was blue, clear, and clean. The trees were covered with blue snow, and the bay was pure blue ice. The sky was blue. The ground was blue. And everything was quite still . . .

30 And then Paul Bunyan saw a great wall of blue ice moving across the bay. And in the ice, there was a creature.

Paul hurried forward and pulled the animal from the ice. It was an ox calf. Paul thought it was only a few hours old. A newborn calf, frozen stiff, unable to move by itself . . . and it was bright blue!

35   Paul pulled the calf out of the ice. "Poor baby," he said. He held the calf close to his chest. The calf opened one eye and looked at him. It was very weak. Paul carried it back to his cave. "Poor baby," he said again.

    All that day and all that night Paul Bunyan worked on the calf.
40 He put it near the fire in his cave. He rubbed it to make its blood flow. He talked to the calf, saying "Come on, Babe! Get strong! You can do it!"

    And in the morning, Babe the blue calf stood up. It was enormous! It was like a blue building! But the poor blue calf could
45 not stand up for very long.

    Babe the blue calf was still weak, so Paul Bunyan gathered some food. All day he fed the calf, and by nightfall the baby ox was well.

    And so Paul Bunyan took care of the baby calf and Babe grew, and grew, and grew. Babe grew so large that they could no longer
50 stay in the cave. It grew so large that the distance between its eyes was forty-two ax handles and one plug of tobacco. It grew so long that a man could not see from its head to its tail.

    So now Paul the giant had a giant blue ox to help him. But what could they do?

55   Paul worried and wondered. He was such a strong man! And Babe was such a huge ox! He should do something special!

> *1. What can very strong people do that other people cannot?*
> *2. Do you know what <u>logging</u> is? Are these descriptions true?*
>> *a. Cutting trees into logs, which are thick pieces of wood.*
>> *b. Moving those big logs so people can build houses.*

    Paul and Babe were standing on a hill. Paul was wondering what to do. He picked up a tree to scratch his ear, and he had an idea.

    He and Babe were very big and very strong. They could move
60 anything. They could even move the great trees of the forest.

    Paul Bunyan knew what to do.

    Paul Bunyan said, "I will invent logging. I will cut the trees and make them into logs. Babe will carry them. People will use the trees to build their houses."

> *3. Look at the map on page 39. Can you find Lake Superior, the*
>> *Mississippi River, and the Grand Canyon? How big are they?*

65   Now these are the things people say about Paul Bunyan.

       They say he brought water from Lake Superior. Well, Paul tied Babe to a huge container, and Babe dragged the container. You see, Paul wanted the water in North Dakota.

       They say the lakes in Minnesota were made by Babe's hoofs
70 sinking into the ground.

       They say that one time Babe slipped and the water tank turned over. That's how the Mississippi River started.

       They say Paul let his peavey, a pole with a sharp spike on the end, drag behind him. That's how the Grand Canyon began. And
75 they say that Babe pushed up some hills, and that made the Cascade range of mountains.

       Don't believe a word of it!

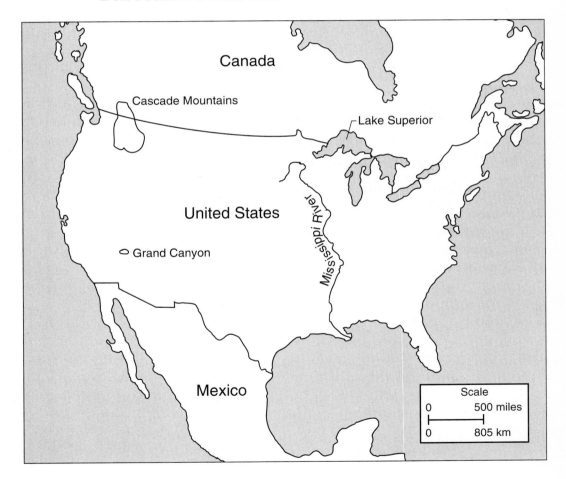

AFTER THE STORY

A. Work with a classmate and answer this question.

Do you believe this story? Underline *Yes* if you do, *No* if you do not. Then give reasons for your answer.

     Yes   No

B. Read the story again. Look at the picture. Work with a classmate, and try to guess the meaning of the words you don't know. If you can't guess, you may look in the dictionary.

C. Now answer these questions.

1. Put these events in order. We did the first one for you.

    a. ___ Paul Bunyan looked out of his cave and saw the blue snow.

    b. _1_ The blue snow fell all night.

    c. ___ Paul wondered what he and Babe could do.

    d. ___ Paul Bunyan looked after the calf all night.

    e. ___ Paul decided to invent logging.

    f. ___ Babe got better, and grew, and grew, and grew.

    g. ___ Paul found the blue ox in the ice.

2. Go through the story and underline all the places where there is an exaggeration. (An exaggeration is when something is made to sound much bigger or taller than it really is.) We found the first one for you. It's in line 13: The cave was big enough to hold a city.

D. Match the words with their meanings. We did the first one for you.

1. cave
2. snowflakes
3. carpet
4. weak
5. beard
6. calf
7. container
8. hoof

a. something you put things into
b. a baby ox
c. not strong
d. covering for the floor
e. deep, hollow place in a mountain
f. tiny pieces of snow
g. hair that men grow on their faces
h. an ox's foot

E. Think about the story. Work with a classmate.

1. Scan the story and find where it says the distance between Babe the Blue Ox's eyes. Write the line number here: _____.

2. Look back at the predictions your group made at the beginning of the story. Compare them with what happened in the story.

3. Did you think this story was funny? What were the funny parts? Why? With a classmate, look back through the story to help you decide. Talk with your classmate and write your answers below:

_____

_____

_____

_____

4. What sort of woman would love Paul Bunyan?

F. Talk about these things with your classmates.

1. A tall tale is a story nobody will believe, like the story of Paul Bunyan and Babe the Blue Ox. Do people tell tall tales in your home country? Can you tell one? Tell it to the class, or write it down. These notes may help you.
   - Tell the name of the story, and tell when and where it happened.
   - Tell who the people are in the story.

- Tell what happened first, second, and third.
- Tell how the story ended.

2. Make up exaggerations about things, like saying a cat is as big as a lion. Write them on the chalkboard.

BEYOND THE STORY

G. Do these activities.

1. Go to the library and find more stories about Paul Bunyan. Share what you learn with your teacher and classmates.

2. Talk with your classmates about these questions:
Why do you think people love stories about good, kind, gentle giants? What could a cruel giant do?

3. Answer this question. What job could Paul Bunyan do today? Be ready to explain your answers to the rest of the class.

4. Do a mime. How would it feel to be a giant? Pretend you are very, very large. How do you walk through a door, sit in a chair . . . ?

TWO POEMS

The men who cut the wood were called lumbermen, or shanty boys, and their lives were very hard. Here are two poems about them. The first is from Kemp P. Battle, *Great American Folklore,* published by Simon & Schuster, Inc.

Find out what these words mean before you read the poems.

| conceal | earn | pastime | hunt |
| buck | doe | sleighs | campfire |

THE LUMBERMAN'S SONG

When the white frost takes the valley
    And the snow conceals the woods,
Each farmer has enough to do
    To earn the family food.
With the week no better pastime
    Than to hunt the buck and doe
And we'll range the wildwoods over
    And once more a-lumbering go.

You may talk about your farms
    Your houses and fine ways,
And pity us poor shanty boys
    While dashing in our sleighs:
While round a good campfire at night
    We'll sing while the wild winds blow,
And we'll range the wildwoods over
    And once more a-lumbering go.

H. Think about the poem.

1. What pleasures does the poet talk about?

2. This poem is called a song. Do you think people could sing it?

3. Ask the other people in your class how they feel when they read the poem.

The other poem is from *A Treasury of American Folklore*, edited by B. A. Botkin, published by Bonanza Books, New York. It tells how a young lumberman died.

Lumbermen put the logs on the river to float down to the towns. Sometimes the logs got caught on something in the river and would not move. This was called a logjam. It was very dangerous to break the logjam because the logs were large and heavy. Once they were free, they rushed down the river.

4. Before you read the poem, match these words to their meanings. We did the first one for you.

1. youth   a. place you are buried
2. genteel   b. empty
3. grave   c. young man
4. morn   d. head of a team of workers
5. void   e. morning
6. foreman   f. polite, well-behaved

GERRY'S ROCKS

Come all ye true-born shanty boys, whoever that ye be,
I would have you pay attention and listen unto me.
Concerning a young shanty-boy, so tall, genteel and brave,
'Twas on a jam on Gerry's rocks he met a watery grave.

It happened on a Sunday morn as you shall quickly hear.
Our logs were piled up mountain high, no one could keep them clear.
Our boss he cried, "Turn out, brave boys, your hearts are void of fear!
We'll break that jam on Gerry's rocks, and for Agonston we'll steer."

They had not rolled off many logs when the boss to them did say,
"I'd have you be on your guard, brave boys. That jam will soon give way."
But scarce the warning had he spoke when the jam did break and go,
It carried away those six brave youths and their foreman, young Monroe.

5. Retell the story of what happened to young Monroe. Write it like a newspaper report.
   - Make up a headline.
   - Tell where the story happened, who was in the story, what Monroe's job was, and what sort of person he was.
   - Tell what happened to him.

6. How do you feel when you read this poem?

7. Which poem do you like better? Why?

5

JOHN LUTHER ("CASEY") JONES
1864–1900

Casey Jones worked on the railroads. Men like John Henry made tunnels through the mountains and built the railroad tracks. When the tracks were ready, other people came to make the trains run. There were people to clean the trains. There were people to make sure the trains were working properly, and there were the engineers.

Casey Jones worked on the railroads as an engineer, driving the trains. Thirty years had passed since John Henry worked on the tunnel. Now the trains carried people and goods across America. It was very important that the train arrive on time, and the engineers hated to run late.

At the end of the nineteenth century, the trains provided the fastest and easiest way to move things. There were no airplanes, and the roads were very bad. There were no cars, and people used horses to carry loads or to travel long distances. It is not surprising that the trains were very important to the people scattered in small settlements across the United States.

The trains made the people feel less alone. When they heard the train go by, they knew there was a way to get to be with other people.

CASEY JONES AND ENGINE NUMBER 638

BEFORE THE STORY

Talk to your classmates. Be ready to tell your teacher what other people in your group said.

1. Look at the pictures on page 48. Then answer these questions.

    a. What do you see?

    b. How old is the man? Describe him.

    c. What sort of person is he?

    d. Write the other students' comments here:

    _____

    _____

    _____

    _____

    e. When do you think the pictures of Casey and the engine were taken?

    f. Have you ever seen an engine like this? Do you know what makes it run? Underline your guess.

        diesel   fuel   gasoline   electricity   coal

    g. How did people keep the train going?

    h. What is in the container directly behind the engine?

2. Try to say what these words mean.

        telegraph   operator   signal   railroads   freight cars

        siding   carriages   brakes   valve   train wreck

3. Show your teacher what these words mean.

        powerful   whistle   steep   ache   explode   leap   yell

4. Read page 51 and find out what Mrs. Jones said about Casey. The information is on lines ___ to ___.

5. Now read page 52, lines 56–65. The passage begins, "Sometimes Casey Jones did things . . ." What do the other people in your group expect to happen? Make a note of what they predict.

_____

_____

_____

_____

_____

6. **Now read the story once, or listen while your teacher reads. Don't worry if you don't understand all the words when you first read a story. Just try to get the main idea.**

CASEY JONES AND ENGINE NUMBER 638

In 1890 Casey Jones was an engineer on the Illinois Central Railroad line. He had worked for the railroads all his life. Casey's first job in the railroads was as a telegraph operator. It was his job to make sure that the engineers driving the trains got the messages about the track ahead of the train. If the railroad track was broken, the engineer had to know. Casey sent the signals that passed up and down the line. It was important work, but it did not require much movement, and Casey loved to move around.

Later, Casey became a brakeman. It was his job to look after the rear part of the train and to put on the brakes which controlled the movement of the load. He stopped the carriages and freight cars from rolling when the engine stopped.

Casey married Miss Janie Brodie in 1887, when she was eighteen. Twenty-eight years after his death she remembered him as being lovable and good humored, a man who always smiled. He had gray eyes and dark hair. He laughed a lot and enjoyed being with people. In those days most men drank alcohol, but Casey did not, and this made him unusual.

Casey was not his real name. His parents named him John Luther Jones, but people called him Casey because he came from a town with a name that sounded like Casey. Casey was a nickname.

After he was married, Casey became a fireman. There were two men in the cabin of the old steam trains: the engineer who drove the train and the fireman. The fireman threw coal into the fire to boil the water which drove the train. The engine got its power from boiling water in a huge boiler. The steam came from the hot water and drove the wheels.

Coal is heavy, and the fireman worked for hours at a time. Casey was a powerful man. He stood six feet four inches tall and was strongly built, but even he ached at the end of a journey.

At last, in 1890, Casey became an engineer and rode on the right-hand side of the engine's cab. He loved his job and he was very good at it. The train needed to stop for coal and for water, but a good engineer could make his fuel and water last. Casey Jones was a very good engineer: he never wasted fuel and he never wasted water.

And then, in 1893, he went to Chicago to an exhibition of trains, and he saw Engine 638. It was love at first sight. Casey

admired the strong, heavy engine. He checked its wheels and climbed into the cabin. He looked at the controls and checked the
40   size of the boiler for the steam. He knew he must have this engine!

Finally, the railroad company let Casey have Engine 638. Casey was delighted with the engine's speed and power, and he drove his train as fast as it would go. He didn't worry very much about safety. Even if he had to lose time and wait in a siding for the tracks to be
45   clear, Casey was rarely late. But sometimes he drove so fast it was dangerous, and that was a reckless thing to do.

Each engine had its own whistle. The whistle on Engine 638 had six thin tubes bound together. When Casey let the steam through it, the whistle made its own special sound. Everybody who heard it
50   knew that Casey Jones was rushing past on the 638.

Casey Jones's fireman was called Sim Webb. The two men were used to working together, and they took pride in their work. They were never late: Casey Jones and Sim Webb always arrived at the advertised time. They were punctual, and they kept to their
55   schedule.

Sometimes Casey Jones did things which were against the rules of the railroad. There is one story about the time Casey was trying to make his engine go up a very steep hill. The other engineers always used two engines to pull a load up this hill, but Casey used only one
60   engine, his beloved 638. But he did something dangerous. There was a gauge which showed how much pressure the steam was under. Casey Jones screwed it down. Now the engine seemed to be using the right amount of pressure, but really it was using twenty pounds more. It was quite possible that the boiler would explode.

65   Casey was lucky, and 638 did not blow up. But Casey loved speed, and he was quite happy to take a risk and to trust to luck.

Casey loved to make the engine go as fast as it could, roaring along the track. He loved to use his whistle so people would say, "There goes Casey Jones."

> *What do you think will happen?*
> *Is it dangerous to speed?*
> *Will Casey Jones always be able to take such risks?*

70   At ten o'clock on Sunday night, April 29, 1900, Casey Jones and Sim Webb were getting ready to go home. They had brought a train

from Canton to Memphis, and they were at the railroad office to hand in their papers.

The clerk in the office said, "One of the other drivers can't go out tonight. He's sick. We'll have to cancel the train. It just can't go."

"You can't do that," said Casey.

"I'm afraid I'll have to," the clerk said.

"I'll take it out," Casey said. He turned to his fireman. "What do you say, Sim?"

"Sure," Sim replied. So both men hurried to the train. It was not Casey's 638, but Number 382. Casey got Number 382 going quickly.

"We're running behind time," Casey said. "The other driver was sick, so we left the station ninety-five minutes late." He looked at the gauges. "It's risky," he said, "but I'm going to push the engine along as quickly as I can."

Sim threw coal onto the fire, and Casey opened the throttle and let the engine go as fast as possible. The train rushed through the countryside.

At 3:50 A.M. Casey and Sim were only two minutes behind schedule. "We're catching up. With any luck we'll get there on time," Sim said. "We sure are going fast!"

Casey just grinned. He loved speed.

Then Sim said, "Look up ahead!"

Casey looked. There was a long freight train in the siding. It was too long for the siding, and the end of it stuck out onto Casey's line. Casey hit the brakes to slow his train down.

"Jump, Sim, and save yourself," Casey ordered. Sim saw the other train coming closer and closer as they raced toward it.

Look back at the predictions your group made after reading lines 53–64. Ask the other students if they want to change anything.

The engine was slowing a little, but Casey knew what was going to happen. "Jump!" he yelled. Sim leaped from the train.

Casey Jones stayed in the engine. He put the brake on and he blew the engine's whistle to warn people. The train slowed down to about thirty-five miles per hour. Then, at 3:52 A.M. on April 30, 1900, Casey's engine plowed into the end of the train in the siding . . .

Sim Webb fell into some bushes. He was not hurt.

When they found Casey Jones, he was dead. He had one hand on the whistle and the other on the brake. He was the only person to die in that terrible wreck. People said he was a hero who saved everyone else. The railroad company said that Casey caused the

110   accident. But still today, when people talk about Casey Jones, they talk about a brave engineer.

AFTER THE STORY

A. Work with a classmate, and answer this question. What happened? Underline the correct answer.

    1. Casey Jones jumped from the train in time.

    2. Casey Jones died in the wreck of train 382.

    3. Casey Jones hated being a railroad engineer.

B. Read the story again. Look at the pictures. Work with a classmate, and try to guess the meaning of words you don't know. If you can't guess, you may look in the dictionary.

C. Now answer these questions.

1. Who is likely to say these things? Match these speakers with the quotations. We did the first one for you.

1. Casey Jones	a. He told me to jump, and that saved my life.
2. Janie Brodie Jones	b. I love my engine, number 638!
3. the railroad company	c. We'll have to cancel the train.
4. Sim Webb	d. My Casey laughed a lot.
5. the clerk in the office	e. Jones was a reckless engineer who loved speed and caused a wreck.

2. Look back through the story and fill out this form. We did the first line for you.

> Year: *1890*
>
> 1. Name: *Casey Jones*
>
> 2. Age:
>
> 3. Occupation:
>
> 4. Height:
>
> 5. Color of eyes:
>
> 6. Color of hair:
>
> 7. Marital status (underline one):　　married　　widowed
>   　　　　　　　　　　　　　　　　single　　divorced
>
> 8. Previous work on railroads (underline jobs he has done, or is doing):
>
>   telegraph operator　　engine wiper　　cleaner
>
>   porter　　guard　　brakeman　　fireman
>
>   engineer

D. Look at these words and phrases, and underline the one in each row which has a different meaning. We did the first one for you.

1. explode　　　　blow up　　　　<u>crash</u>
2. be careful　　　take risks　　　trust to luck
3. arriving early　　running behind　running late
4. slow down　　　rush　　　　　hurry
5. punctual　　　　late　　　　　on time
6. dangerous　　　risky　　　　　safe
7. smile　　　　　laugh　　　　　grin
8. jump　　　　　leap　　　　　fall

E. People said Casey Jones was a hero who saved everyone else. However, the railroad company claimed that Casey had not been careful and that his love of speed caused the wreck. What do you think? Look back at the story with your partner. Then ask your classmates this question.

Did Casey Jones cause the wreck? Write your answers here.

Name of student   Yes /No   Reason for answer

_____

_____

_____

_____

_____

F. Work with your classmates.

1. Pretend you are Sim Webb, and tell the railroad bosses what happened. Another member of the class can pretend to be a railroad boss. You may make notes *before* you speak, but don't just read from them.

2. Work with your partner or group and prepare a summary of the story. Be ready to read it aloud or to write it on the chalkboard. The class will choose the best summary.

3. Have you ever driven very quickly? How did it make you feel? Were other people with you? How did they feel?

BEYOND THE STORY

G. Now do these activities.

1. Go to the library and find out more about Casey Jones. Find out about the railroads 100 years ago. What has changed? Share what you learn with your teacher and your classmates.

2. Think about the different jobs Casey did on the railroads. Ask your classmates which one they would like most? Which one would they like least? Why?

3. How much responsibility does a worker have for safety at work? How much responsibility does the employer have? Think of an accident at work that you know about, and discuss the problem with your group.

THE BALLAD OF CASEY JONES

Before you read the song, here are some explanations.

- A rounder was a wandering railway worker.
- A right-wheeler was an engine driver who rode on the right side of the cabin.
- "You got a white eye," may mean "You have a signal which is against you."
- "'Twas" is an abbreviation of "it was."
- A moan is a quiet sound usually made by a person or an animal in pain.
- A ballad is a song which tells a story.

THE BALLAD OF CASEY JONES

Come all you rounders if you want to hear
The story of a brave engineer;
Casey Jones was the rounder's name,
A high right-wheeler of mighty fame.

Through the South Memphis yards on the fly
He heard the firemen say, "You got a white eye."
All the people knew by the engine's moans
That the man at the throttle was Casey Jones.

Casey says, "Fireman, don't you fret.
Keep knocking at the fire door: don't give up yet.
I'm going to run her till she leaves the rail
Or make it on time with the southern mail."

"'Twas round the curve he saw a passenger train.
Something happened in Casey's brain.
Fireman jumped off, but Casey stayed on.
He's a good engineer, but he's dead and gone—

Headaches and heartaches and all kinds of pain
Are not apart from a railroad train.
Tales that are earnest, noble and grand
Belong to the life of a railroad man.

H. Think about the song.

1. What do you think "Keep knocking at the fire door" means?

2 Have you ever heard a steam train? What sound does it make? What sound do its wheels make? Tell the class.

3. What do these lines make you hear?

> *All the people knew by the engine's moans*
> *That the man at the throttle was Casey Jones.*

4 If you have ridden in a steam train, tell the class about it. Tell them what you enjoyed and what you disliked. Compare your ride with a ride on another sort of train.

6

DAVID CROCKETT
1786–1836

David Crockett was a very popular leader in America early in the nineteenth century. Although you will often see him called "Davy Crockett," he always used his full name, David. In stories he is nearly always called "Davy."

David Crockett was popular because people thought he was just like them. He told stories about his own mistakes and about his own wrongdoings.

This story tells how Davy Crockett got into Congress, which is part of the government of the United States.

CROCKETT MAKING A CHARACTERISTIC CANVASS. (245)

DAVY CROCKETT AND THE COONSKIN

BEFORE THE STORY

Talk to your classmates. Be ready to tell your teacher what other people in your group said.

1. Look at the picture of the crowd on page 60. It comes from *Davy Crockett, Gentleman from the Cane.* It was published by the Smithsonian Institution and the Tennessee State Museum.

   Now answer these questions.

   a. What do you and the people in your group see? Describe the picture.

   b. What do you think the man is saying?

   c. Why do you think there are there no women in the picture?

   d. Is this a modern picture? What time does this picture illustrate? Underline the correct answer.

   > between 1800 and 1850   between 1850 and 1900
   > between 1900 and 1950

   Why did you choose your answer? Look at page 59 to see when Davy Crockett was alive.

   e. What is happening in the picture on page 61? What is Davy Crockett doing with the coonskin? Does the man behind the bar know? Look at the two pictures. What do you think happens in this story? Make notes of what your group decides. Your story may be just as good as the one in this book.

2. Now answer these questions.

   a. What do you know about the Congress of the United States?

   b. Do you know what "to vote" means?

   c. How do people get to be Congressmen or Congresswomen?

3. Try to say what these words mean.

   > elect   election   leader   candidate   opponent   trick

4. Show the teacher what these words mean.

    a crack   a wink   shoot   thirsty   taste

5. Do you know what a raccoon is?

6. **Now read the story once, or listen while your teacher reads. Don't worry if you don't understand all the words when you first read a story. Just try to get the main idea.**

DAVY CROCKETT AND THE COONSKIN

Davy Crockett wanted to be a leader of his people. He wanted to serve in the Congress of the United States. But first, he had to get people to vote for him. So he tried to make people think that he was a good leader. He wanted the people to like him.

Davy Crockett had an opponent. This was another man who wanted to get into Congress. Davy's opponent was busy talking to a group of men. "If you vote for me," he said, "I promise I will do good things for you."

Davy Crockett climbed up onto a stump outside a store. He began to talk to anyone who would listen. Slowly the crowd drifted over to listen to him. Davy told them how good he was, how truthful, how brave. They listened for a while, and then one man said, "That's all very well. We've listened to you for a long time. Now take us into the saloon and buy us a drink."

"Yes," they all said, "we've listened long enough. We're thirsty. It's time for some rum."

Now, back in those days very few people carried money. They traded things instead. A good knife was worth a bag of flour, or a cow cost a gun; if you gave me your gun, you could have my cow. Like most people, Davy Crockett had no money. But he did want to go to Congress, and to do that, he had to buy liquor for the crowd.

Everyone crowded into the saloon, which was also the general store. In those days, the store sold everything: clothing, food, animal skins, and, of course, liquor.

The man who ran this store was mean. His name was Job Snelling, and he never gave anything away. Job said nobody could steal from him. He said he never closed his eyes, not even when he was asleep.

Do you think that Job Snelling will let Davy Crockett have rum without paying for it?

The men crowded into the store.

Job Snelling said, "What can I do for you?"

Davy Crockett spoke to Job. "Will you let me have a quart of your best rum?" he asked politely.

"Do you have any money?" Job asked.

35 "No," Davy Crockett said, "I don't have any today. But I'll pay you later. Trust me."

Job pointed to a sign over the bar. It said, "Pay today and trust later."

All the men turned to look at Davy Crockett. Davy Crockett
40 stood up tall, and turned toward the door. Everyone followed him out of the store.

"You wait here," Crockett told them. He marched off into the woods.

"What's he going to do?" somebody asked.

45 "He's going to shoot something," his friend replied. "Davy Crockett is a great shot. Just wait. He'll bring something back."

Just then there was a bang! Davy Crockett had shot a raccoon. He walked back into the clearing and skinned the raccoon. Then he said to the waiting men, "Come on! We'll go back to Job's."

50 So they all went back to Job's store. "We've come back for our liquor," Davy Crockett said, and he put the skin on the counter. "Give me a quart of your best, and take the skin to pay for it."

Job looked at the skin. It was worth money because there were no holes in it. Job Snelling took the skin and gave Davy Crockett the
55 quart of rum.

The men passed the bottle around. They drank from it, and they laughed and grew merry.

"Old Job makes a good rum," one man said.

"I bet it's just corncob and molasses," another man said. "But it
60 tastes good. It hits the spot. Get us some more, Colonel Crockett."

Davy Crockett had no more money. How could he buy more liquor?

Then he saw the coonskin. Job had pushed it into a crack between the logs under the bar. Davy could just reach it.

65 Job was looking the other way. Quick as a wink, Davy Crockett grabbed the coonskin.

"Another quart of your best," he said.

"How are you going to pay?" Job asked.

Davy didn't say anything. He gave the coonskin to Job. Job
70 quickly pushed it back into the crack.

*What will happen if Job catches Davy Crockett stealing
the coonskin?*

What will the other people think of Davy Crockett's trick?

Soon the men were drinking again. They agreed that Colonel Crockett was the man for them.

Davy Crockett used that coonskin eight times more. Everyone knew what he was doing. Everyone, that is, except Job.

75 The men all decided that Davy Crockett was the man to send to Congress. They said if he could fool Job, he could trick anyone.

And that's how Davy Crockett got elected to Congress.

After the election Davy Crockett went to see Job. Job was ready for him.

80 "I found that one coonskin," Job said. "You sold it to me ten times."

"Yes, sir, I did," Davy Crockett said. "And I'm here to pay you."

Job laughed. "Don't worry," he said.

Davy Crockett was very surprised.

85 "Well, you got my vote," Job said. "Anyone who can trick me is very smart. Anyway, I added the cost of your rum to the price I charged your opponent."

Davy Crockett laughed. "You mean you made the man running against me pay for my rum?"

90 "That's right," Job said. "He was a fool. He doesn't deserve to get into Congress. We need smart men there to look after things for us. You'll do. In any case, it's good for a man like me to get fooled every now and again. It keeps me sharp. But don't try to fool me again, because I'm ready for you."

95 And how do we know this story? David Crockett told it himself! The story, and stories like it, appear in *The Life and Adventures of Colonel David Crockett of West Tennessee*, published in 1833.

AFTER THE STORY

A. Work with a classmate, and answer this question: How did Davy Crockett pay for his rum? Underline the correct answer.

1. He paid with money.

2. He paid with ten raccoon skins.

3. He paid with the same raccoon skin ten times.

B. Read the story again. Look at the pictures. Work with a classmate, and try to guess the meaning of the words you don't know. If you can't guess, you may look in the dictionary.

C. Now answer these questions.

1. Put these events in order. We did the first one for you.
   a. ____ Davy stole the raccoon skin back, and he used it to pay Job.
   b. ____ Davy Crockett used the raccoon skin to pay Job.
   c. ____ Davy Crockett took everyone into the saloon.
   d. ____ Davy Crockett had no money, so he shot a raccoon.
   e. ____ Job Snelling said that Davy Crockett had to pay.
   f. ____ Job put the raccoon skin in a place where Davy could get it.
   g. ____ Later, Job said that Davy did not have to pay.
   h. _1_ Davy Crockett tried to talk to the crowd, but they said they wanted rum.

2. Who is likely to say these things. Match the speakers with the quotation. We did the first one for you.

   1. Davy Crockett's opponent
   2. Job Snelling
   3. Davy Crockett

   a. I know he tricked me with the coonskin. It's good for me to be fooled sometimes.
   b. I want to get into Congress. Vote for me. I'm better than Crockett!
   c. I need money to buy rum for the people. What can I do? I don't have any money!
   d. I'll shoot something and sell the skin to Job.
   e. I have a motto: Pay now and trust later.
   f. I wonder why this liquor bill is so high?
   g. I made Davy's opponent pay for the liquor.

D. See if you can do this crossword puzzle.

Across

2. to express a choice on who you want to do something

3. a person who leads

5. describes someone who is not willing to share or help

6. a place where you buy things

Down

1. the elected law-making body of the United States

4. to choose somebody by voting

7. to deceive somebody

E. Work with a classmate.

1. With a partner, complete the grid below. If you think someone has the quality, put a plus sign (+) in the grid. If you don't know, put a zero in the space. If they lack the quality, put a minus sign (−) there. For instance, Job Snelling is mean, so we gave him a minus under Generous.

	Clever	Generous	Honest	Quick-thinking
Davy Crockett				
Job Snelling		−		
Crockett's opponent				

2. What do you think of Davy Crockett? Can you understand why people liked him? Do you think the story is funny? With a classmate, look back through the story to help you see Davy more clearly. Discuss Davy Crockett with your classmate, and write your ideas below.

_____

_____

_____

_____

_____

F. Talk about the story.

1. Look back at the predictions your group made before the story. Do you like your story better than the one in this book? Write your story so you can share it with the class.

_____

_____

_____

_____

_____

2. Talk about these things with your classmates.

   Do you know any stories about people who trick other people? Can you make up a story? These notes may help you.
   - Tell where the story happened, and when.
   - Tell who the people in the story are.
   - Tell what happened first, second, and third.
   - Tell what the result or conclusion of the story was.

3. Did Davy Crockett do a morally good thing? Why was he proud of it? Why do we find it funny? Discuss this with your classmates.

BEYOND THE STORY

G. Now do these activities.

1. Go to the library and find out more about Davy Crockett. Share what you learn with your classmates and your teacher.

2. Ask your teacher or the librarian for the words of "The Ballad of Davy Crockett." It begins, "Born on a mountain top in Tennessee . . ." and was a very popular song in the 1950s. Why do you think people liked it?

3. Find out about the Congress of the United States. Then try to find answers to these questions.
   a. What electoral district is your school in?
   b. Who is the representative?
   c. What party does he or she belong to?
   d. What can he or she do for your district?
   e. See if you can find any news about the representative for the class bulletin board.

SONG: THE DODGER

Before you read the song, here are some explanations.

- A dodger is someone who changes to suit the times and is not quite honest.
- To treat someone is to buy things for them, usually food and drink.
- A note may refer to money, or it may be a vote.
- This song was not written about Davy Crockett.

THE DODGER

Yes the candidate's a dodger, a well-known dodger;
Yes the candidate's a dodger, and I'm a dodger too.
He'll meet you and treat you and ask you for your vote,
But look out boys, he's a-dodging for a note!

Anonymous

H. Think about the song.

1. Do you think Davy Crockett was like the candidate in the song? Explain your answer.

_____

_____

_____

_____

2. What do you think Davy Crockett would say about the song?

DAVY CROCKETT AND PEG-LEG HUNTSMAN

BEFORE THE STORY

Talk to your classmates. Be ready to tell your teacher what other people in your group said.

1. Look at the picture on page 72. What do you see? Will the chair make a noise? What will it sound like? Describe what is happening.

2. Write your group's prediction of what happens in this story.

3. Now answer these questions. Ask the members of your group to explain their answers.

   a. What do you and your group already know about Davy Crockett? Should anyone trust him?

   b. How would you feel if you met Davy Crockett at a party?

   c. How would you feel if you had to do business with him?

4. Show your teacher what these words mean.

wooden	asleep	snore	creep	grab
fright	thump	stride	bump	

5. A peg-leg is a wooden leg. When people walk with a wooden leg, what sound would it make?

6. **Now read the story once, or listen while your teacher reads. Don't worry if you don't understand all the words when you first read a story. Just try to get the main idea.**

DAVY CROCKETT AND PEG-LEG HUNTSMAN

You remember that in the last story Davy tricked Job Snelling. This is a story about another trick.

Davy Crockett was trying to get elected again. It was 1833, and Davy was running against a man called Adam Huntsman.
5 Huntsman was known as Peg-Leg because he had one wooden leg.

One night both Crockett and Huntsman were staying at the home of a wealthy farmer. The farmer wanted to vote for Huntsman, but he let Davy Crockett stay at his house. It was a long way to the next place where a person could sleep.
10 The men sat around, laughing and talking politics until late at night. The rich farmer was absolutely sure he would vote for Peg-Leg. Davy was worried. He needed every vote he could get. At last they said good night and went to bed.

Davy and Peg-Leg were sharing a room. The farmer's daughter
15 was sleeping in another room at the end of a long wooden porch.

Davy listened carefully. Peg-Leg began to snore. Davy crept out of bed and found a wooden chair. Then he moved quietly along the porch until he arrived outside the young woman's bedroom.

Davy looked around. Nobody was looking. Everyone else in the
20 house was asleep. Peg-Leg was still snoring loudly.

Davy grabbed the door handle and began to turn it. The farmer's daughter woke up and called out "Who's there?" She was frightened.

Davy rattled the door handle again. The farmer's daughter
25 screamed.

Davy could hear the farmer moving around. It was time to go!

Davy took the chair by the back and thumped his way back to his own room. The banging of the chair sounded exactly like somebody walking with a wooden leg.

What will the farmer think?

30 The farmer was up now. Davy could hear him talking to his daughter.

"Somebody tried to get into my room, Father," she said.

"I know," the farmer said angrily. "And I know who it was, too." He strode quickly along the porch to the room where Davy Crockett
35 and Peg-Leg Huntsman were staying.

Huntsman lay asleep. Davy Crockett pretended to be asleep. He snored loudly.

The farmer burst into the room and shook Huntsman awake.

"What were you doing near my daughter?" the farmer asked

40 angrily.

"Huh? What?" poor Peg-Leg Huntsman replied. He was still half asleep.

"Don't try to pretend you're asleep," the farmer said. "I heard you. I heard that old peg-leg of yours bumping along the porch."

45 And no matter what poor Huntsman said, the farmer was sure that Huntsman had tried to get into his daughter's room. The next day the farmer told all his friends about Peg-Leg Huntsman, and they all decided to vote for Davy Crockett.

Do you think people will be fooled forever?

Davy Crockett found it very hard not to laugh, and he couldn't

50 resist talking about his clever trick. By 1835 everyone knew about it. The farmer was angry because Davy had made him look silly. Peg-Leg Huntsman was an honest man, and people decided that Davy's trick was not really very funny. The voters began to wonder if they wanted a trickster like Crockett in the Congress. When the next

55 election came, later in 1835, people voted for Peg-Leg Huntsman, and Davy Crockett lost.

AFTER THE STORY

A. Work with a classmate, and answer this question. How did Davy trick the farmer? Underline the right answer.

1. By telling him stories

2. By making a noise which sounded like a wooden leg

3. By making him drunk

B. Read the story again. Look at the picture. Work with a classmate, and try to guess the meaning of the words you don't know. If you can't guess, you may look in the dictionary.

C. Say whether these statements are true or false. Check under *True* or *False*. If the statement is false, write the correct answer below. We did the first one for you.

	True	False
1. Davy Crockett did not want to be elected again. *Davy Crockett wanted to be elected.*		✔
2. Adam Huntsman had a wooden leg.		
3. Adam Huntsman woke the farmer's daughter.		
4. Davy Crockett went to sleep before Huntsman.		
5. Davy Crockett stayed in his bed all night.		

D. Circle the letter of the sentence which has the same meaning. We did the first one for you.

1. Davy was running against a man with a wooden leg.
   a. They were in a running race.
   b. They both wanted to get elected to Congress.

2. When people are talking politics, they are
   a. talking about politics.
   b. not interested in what is going on.

3. Davy and Peg-Leg were sharing a room.
   a. They were in different rooms.
   b. They were both in the same room.

4. The farmer burst into the room.
   a. He broke the room.
   b. He came into the room very quickly.

E. Work with a classmate.

1. Go through the story with a partner and find things which show what sort of man Davy Crockett was. Then answer these questions.

   a. Why do you think people voted for him?

   b. Why do you think people voted against him?

   c. Would you vote for him?

   d. How do you feel about him?

   Make notes on what you decide.

2. Read this advice which Davy Crockett left us. These are his exact words and punctuation:

   I leave this rule for others when I am dead
   Be always sure, you are right, then go, ahead.

   Now discuss these questions with a classmate. Is it good advice? How can you know you are right? Make notes of your discussion.

F. Talk about the story.

1. Have you ever decided to do something and then just done it?
   - Tell the class, or write your story.
   - Tell what you did and who else was involved.
   - Tell when and where your story happens.
   - Most important, tell why you decided to act and what the result was.

2. Look back at the predictions your group made before the story. How are they different from the story?

BEYOND THE STORY

G. Now do these activities.

1. Pretend you are the farmer, and tell this story.

2. Write a play which tells what happened in the story. Be ready to perform your play for the class.

3. Pretend to interview all the people in the story on radio or television.

4. Go to the library and find out how people are elected to Congress today. When is the next Congressional election? Share what you learn with your classmates and your teacher.

5. There is another Davy Crockett story in the Teacher's Guide. Ask your teacher to tell it to you.

7

CALAMITY JANE
MARTHY JANE CANNARY
1852–1903

Calamity Jane, whose real name was Marthy Jane
Cannary, lived all over the Wild West. She moved around a
lot, but she usually returned to Deadwood, South Dakota.

We don't have many facts about Calamity Jane. She said
she was a scout for the army between 1870 and 1876. But the
army has no records of Calamity Jane. We do know that she
nursed people sick with smallpox in the Black Hills of Dakota
in the late 1870s.

Calamity Jane sang to entertain people, but she drank
too much and lost a lot of jobs. She sometimes shot holes in
buildings, but not in people. She was colorful rather than evil,
and she certainly fits in with the idea of the Wild West.

Calamity Jane died in Deadwood and was buried there.

The story of how Calamity Jane got her name comes
from *The Life and Adventures of Calamity Jane, by Herself,* which
she wrote around 1893.

Calamity Jane, Gen. Crook's Scout.
Copyrighted by H. R. Locke, 1895.

HOW CALAMITY JANE GOT HER NAME

BEFORE THE STORY

Talk to your classmates. Be ready to tell your teacher what other people in your group said.

1. Look at the picture on page 80. Now answer these questions.

   a. What do you and your group see? Ask each other questions about the woman, her clothes, her gun.

   b. What sort of person do you think she was?

   c. When was the picture taken? Underline the correct answer.
      last year   between 1920 and 1970   between 1850 and 1920

   d. Do you think a lot of women wore trousers in Calamity Jane's day?

2. What does *calamity* mean? Why call somebody "Calamity Jane"?

3. What do you think will happen to this woman?

4. Try to say what these words mean.
      brave   soldier   protect   army post
      fort   gallop   troops

5. **Now listen while your teacher reads the story. Close your books.**

HOW CALAMITY JANE GOT HER NAME

Calamity Jane said that she was a brave rider. She told people that she could ride any horse that ran. This is her story of how she got her name. Calamity Jane is speaking.

"It was 1873, and I was twenty-one years old. I was at Goose
5   Creek, Wyoming. Captain Egan was the soldier in command of the army post.

"I was in a party of soldiers who were protecting the army post. We went out for several days' patrol. We had a lot of small fights with the Indians. Some of our soldiers died and others were badly hurt.

10   "We were riding back to the post when the Indians attacked us. We were a mile and a half from the fort. I was riding at the front of the troops when I heard a shot. I looked around. Captain Egan was falling from his horse!

"I turned my horse around, and galloped back to save him. I
15   caught him as he was falling. I lifted him onto my horse in front of me. I managed to get him safely to the fort.

"When he got better, Captain Egan called me 'Calamity Jane, the heroine of the plains.' The name has stuck to me ever since."

AFTER THE STORY

A. Work with your classmates and answer these questions.

1. Do you believe this story?

2. Why do you think the story is true (or not true)?

B. See if you can explain how the story could be true? Show your classmates.

Calamity Jane's Bet

Before the Story

Talk to your classmates. Be ready to tell your teacher what other people in your group said.

1. Look at the picture on page 84 of Calamity Jane with her horse. Work with your group, and take notes. Now answer these questions. What do you know about Calamity Jane? Ask each other questions about her life, her horse, her clothes, her appearance, and anything else you know from the picture and the previous story. For example, do you think Calamity Jane was a good rider? Why?

2. Try to say what these words mean.

   bar   outrun   witnesses   bystanders   mount (a horse)

3. Answer these questions.

   a. Can horses do tricks? Tell your teacher if you know about any. Do you think a horse will go inside a building?

   b. Do you know what a bet is? What do you know about races? Write the words you think of on the word diagram below.

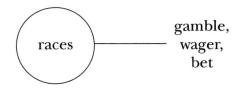

4. What do you think will happen in this story? Write down your group's predictions.

5. Show your teacher what these words mean.

   shiver   pat   flick   jump   mirror

6. **Now read the story once, or listen while your teacher reads. Don't worry if you don't understand all the words when you first read a story. Just try to get the main idea.**

CALAMITY JANE'S BET

Calamity Jane was sitting on her horse in front of a saloon. It was a hot afternoon, and she was wondering what to do. People were laughing and drinking inside the bar.

A stranger rode up. His horse was large and powerful. It had
5 long legs and a strong chest. Calamity Jane looked at it carefully.

"That's a mighty fine horse," she said. "Nearly as fine as my horse, Jim." She patted her horse.

"I'll trade you horses," the stranger said.

Calamity Jane laughed.

10 "Jim is the best horse ever to run," she said. "Why, this horse is the fastest thing on four legs. Why would I exchange him for your horse?"

"My horse could beat your horse any day," the stranger said.

Calamity Jane just laughed sleepily. She didn't bother to say
15 anything.

"I'll bet my horse can outrun your Jim," the stranger said hotly. "Just name the time."

Calamity Jane woke up a little.

"What do you bet?" she asked.

20 "Money, whiskey, whatever you like," the stranger said. "Are you interested? Or is that horse of yours too slow?"

Calamity Jane patted Jim's strong neck.

"Can I decide how far we race?" she asked.

"Of course," the stranger replied. "I'm not worried. My horse'll
25 win anyway."

"Can I choose where we run?"

"Of course. And you can name when we run." The stranger was feeling very safe.

Do you think Calamity Jane has a plan?
Do you think the stranger will win the race? Why?

Calamity Jane yelled into the saloon, "Somebody come out here.
30 We're going to have a race. I need witnesses to the rules of the contest."

Several men came out.

"How much will you wager?" Calamity Jane asked the stranger.

"One hundred dollars, winner takes all."

35 Calamity Jane held her hand out. "Give me the money," she said. The stranger handed it to her. She pulled out $100 of her own and turned to one of the bystanders.

"Ned," she said, "you're an honest man. Hold this. It's $100 of mine and $100 of this gentleman's. Whoever wins the race gets all
40 the money."

Everyone watched as Ned put the money into his pocket.

"When do you want to race?" Ned asked.

"Now," the stranger said eagerly. "Then I can take my $200 and go to the next town."

45 "That's fine," Calamity Jane said. "You said I could choose the course of the race."

"Of course," the stranger said. "You tell me where we run. My horse will still beat your Jim."

Jim gave a shiver when he heard his name, and flicked his tail.
50 Calamity Jane turned to the little crowd and saw a young man in it. "Write this down please, Joe," she said.

Joe got a pencil and paper from the bar of the saloon. "I'm ready," he said.

How do you think the crowd will feel about this race?
Do you think it will be an ordinary race?

"This is the course," Calamity Jane began. "First, we take the
55 horses twenty feet back from the saloon. We jump them up onto the platform in front of the saloon. We ride into the saloon. We take a drink, then we ride out through the back door. Do you think you can do that?"

The stranger said, "My horse can jump onto that platform." He
60 walked around to the back of the saloon. The saloon was not very far off the ground, so the platform was low. "He can jump out again, too. Is that all?"

"That's all," Calamity Jane said. "But we do it in every saloon in town. We go into the next saloon by the back door and out by the
65 front. The third saloon we go in by the front door and out by the back. First horse at the bar of the last saloon wins the money."

"How many saloons are there?" the stranger asked. He looked excited.

70　　　"Eleven, if we include the dance halls," Calamity Jane said calmly.

The crowd looked at the stranger.

"Do you think he's ever ridden through saloons before?" Ned asked the man next to him.

75　　　"Probably," the man replied. "He looks like a saloon-riding man."

Joe finished writing down the rules of the contest. "Do you think he knows that Calamity Jane rides Jim through the saloons once a week?" he asked Ned.

80　　　"Naw," Ned said. "I don't think he knows that."

The two riders mounted their horses. Ned gave the signal, and they were off.

Jim jumped up onto the platform and went into the first saloon. Calamity Jane had a drink, and they went straight out the back door.

85　　The stranger and his horse were right behind them.

Jim was having fun. He knew the bars very well. Calamity Jane just had to sit on his back. But the stranger's horse was having a hard time. It didn't know these bars. The mirrors frightened it. And Jim knew where he was going, the stranger's horse didn't.

90　　　And that's how Calamity Jane won the race. She finished three saloons and four drinks ahead of the stranger.

"Just goes to prove that practice makes perfect," Ned said as he gave Calamity Jane the $200.

AFTER THE STORY

A. Work with a classmate and answer this question. How did Calamity Jane win the race? Underline the correct answer.

1. She made the other horse sick.

2. She named a course which she and her horse ran regularly.

3. She told the other rider the wrong way to go.

B. Read the story again. Look at the picture. Work with a classmate and try to guess the meaning of the words you don't know. If you can't guess, you may look in the dictionary.

C. Match the beginning of these sentences with the most suitable ending. We did the first one for you.

1. Calamity Jane was ————————————
2. The stranger was quite sure
3. Calamity Jane asked if she

4. They decided to race
5. Jim knew the inside
6. The people in the crowd
7. Calamity Jane and Jim

a. could decide how far to race.
b. of all the bars.
c. that his horse was faster than Jim.
d. wondering what to do.
e. for a prize of $100.
f. won the race easily.
g. expected Calamity Jane to win.

D. Study these words and sentences.

1. Look at these words, and underline the word in each row which has a different meaning. We did the first one for you.

   1. saloon   bar   platform
   2. pat   exchange   trade
   3. said   yelled   heard
   4. large   powerful   strong
   5. decide   hold   choose
   6. strangers   bystanders   crowd
   7. give   wager   bet

2. Circle the letter of the sentence which has the same meaning. We did the first one for you.

   1. She didn't bother to say anything.
      a. She didn't speak.
      b. She didn't hear.
   2. And you can name when we run.
      a. You can decide when we race.
      b. You can name the race track.

3. He looks like a saloon-riding man.

    a. He looks tough and experienced.

    b. He looks kind and innocent, like a baby.

4. Ned gave the signal, and they were off.

    a. Ned gave the signal, and the race began.

    b. Ned gave the signal, and they fell off their horses.

5. Practice makes perfect.

    a. Now Calamity Jane is perfect.

    b. If you do something a lot, you'll get good at it.

E. Think about the story.

1. Work with a partner. Pretend you are newspaper reporters, and write the story of Calamity Jane's ride for your paper, *The Wild West Times*. Here are some questions your editor wants you to answer.
   - Who is Calamity Jane?
   - What sort of horse was Jim?
   - Who was in the race?
   - What was the course?
   - Who won? Why?
   - Were the people in the town surprised? What did they say?

2. Work with a classmate to produce a WANTED poster for Calamity Jane. Put her picture on the poster, describe what she looks like, and tell why the police want to catch her.

F. Pretend that Calamity Jane is alive today. What questions would you ask her? What advice would you give her? Be ready to put your advice on the chalkboard for the whole class to discuss.

BEYOND THE STORY

G. Now do these activities.

1. Go to the library and find out about the Wild West. Where was it? Why was it wild? Share what you learn with your classmates and your teacher.

2. Try to find old movies about the Wild West. One is called *Calamity Jane* (Warner Brothers). The Calamity Jane of the film is not very much like the Calamity Jane in these stories.

3. Write a play. Pretend you are the stranger, and tell your family how you lost $100. Perform the play for the class.

SONG: HOME ON THE RANGE

This is a traditional song which talks about the joy of being in wide open spaces. A range is a wide spread of land where cattle feed. Buffalo, deer, and antelope are animals which lived in the wild in North America. Home for many people was little more than a tent, but they loved the country around them.

HOME ON THE RANGE

Oh give me a home where the buffalo roam,
    And the deer and the antelope play;
Where seldom is heard a discouraging word,
    And the skies are not cloudy all day.

Chorus: Home, home on the range
    Where the deer and the antelope play;
Where seldom is heard a discouraging word,
    And the skies are not cloudy all day.

Where the air is so pure, and the zephyrs so free
    The breezes so balmy and light,
That I would not exchange my home on the range
    For all of the cities so bright.

Chorus: Home, home on the range
    Where the deer and the antelope play;
Where seldom is heard a discouraging word,
    And the skies are not cloudy all day.

Anonymous

roam: wander happily
zephyr: a gentle wind
balmy: soft, warm (when referring to weather)

H. Think about poetry.

1. Shut your eyes while someone else reads the words to "Home on the Range." What can you see?

2. Find words which make this verse sound happy. What else gives a happy feeling?

3. Imagine Calamity Jane at home on the range. Describe her surroundings. What would she do?

4. How does this song make you feel? Do you like living in the city or the country?

5. The songwriter loved his home on the range. Tell the class about how you feel when you remember a place you love.

6. We can create a place we love just by thinking about it. Emily Dickinson wrote the following poem in 1896. Before you read the poem, read these explanations. Then listen while your teacher reads the poem. How does it make you feel?
   - A prairie is a wide, treeless, grassy plain. Clover is a small flowering plant which bees love.
   - To be in a revery is to enjoy pleasant dreams while you are awake. People spell it *reverie* now, but Emily Dickinson spelled it *revery*.

TO MAKE A PRAIRIE TAKES ONE CLOVER

To make a prairie takes one clover and one bee
One clover, and a bee,
And revery.
The revery alone will do,
If bees are few.

7. Emily Dickinson could create a prairie from one clover and perhaps a bee. What do you need to make you think of a place? Write a poem about a place you love or a place you hate.

8

ANNIE OAKLEY
PHOEBE ANN OAKLEY MOSES
1860–1926

Annie Oakley's real name was Phoebe Ann Oakley Moses. She was an extremely good shot—she could hit any target with her rifle. A Native American chief, Sitting Bull, called Annie "Little Sure Shot."

She lived at about the same time as Calamity Jane, but she was a very different person. When you read her story, see if you can find out what sort of woman she was.

ANNIE OAKLEY.

Gilbert & Bacon

No. 820 Arch St. & 40 N. 8th St., Phila

White   1261 BROADWAY
          N.Y.

ANNIE OAKLEY, LITTLE SURE SHOT

BEFORE THE STORY

Talk to your classmates. Be ready to tell your teacher what other people in your group said.

1. Look at the pictures on pages 93 and 94. Now answer these questions.

   a. What do you see? Describe this woman.

   b. Ask each other questions about her work, her hobbies, her personality, and her appearance.

   c. Compare these pictures of Annie Oakley with those of Calamity Jane on pages 80 and 84. What differences do you and your group notice? Make notes.

   Read lines 17–20 on page 97. The passage begins, "There's a man called Frank Butler. . . ." Then work with your group, and predict what will happen. Make a note of your group's predictions. Be prepared to find out what other groups predicted.

3. Try to say what these phrases mean.

   to do something for a living   to be in a competition

   to perform

4. Now answer these questions.

   a. What is an entertainer? an orphan? a clay pigeon?

   b. When do we say that a person is a star?

   c. What do you know about shooting? Write the words you think of below.

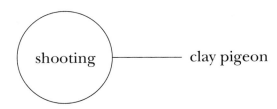

5. Show the teacher what these words and phrases mean.

    hold a dime between your fingers   smoke a cigarette

    jump

6. **Now read the story once, or listen while your teacher reads. Don't worry if you don't understand all the words when you first read a story. Just try to get the main idea.**

Annie Oakley, Little Sure Shot

Phoebe Ann Oakley Moses was born in Darke County, Ohio. Her father died when she was six, and Mrs. Moses had a hard time finding money for the family. When Phoebe was eight, she learned to shoot. She went out and shot birds and animals for a Cincinnati hotel.

The cook at the hotel bought the game that Phoebe shot. "You're a wonderful shot, Miss," he said. "You shoot so well that I never have to take gunshot out of the bodies. You always hit the head."

The money Phoebe earned made life a little easier for the family, but it also brought her fame. Her skill with a gun made people talk about her. People knew about this little girl who used a rifle so well, and they came to see her shoot. By the time she was fifteen she was very well known.

One day in 1875 the owner of the hotel asked Phoebe if she would like to enter a shooting contest.

"There's a man called Frank Butler," he said. "He shoots for a living. In fact, people come to watch him shoot. He can shoot the middle out of a playing card. He's a very good shot, but I think you're better. Will you try? Will you be in the competition?"

Phoebe agreed, and she went to the shooting contest. They were shooting clay pigeons. A clay pigeon is not a real bird. It's just a target which flies through the air. The person who is shooting calls out "Pull!" and someone sends the target into the air.

Phoebe had never shot a clay pigeon before. She was nervous. By contrast, Frank Butler was very calm. He did not believe that Phoebe could win.

Frank Butler was wrong. Phoebe Ann Oakley Moses won the contest, and a year later, she married Frank Butler. She went on the stage and decided to change her name to "Annie Oakley."

Frank and Annie performed in different shows. People came from miles around to watch. Soon Frank could see that most people wanted to see Annie. He became her manager, while she was the star. His job was to look after the business; her job was to show how well she could shoot.

*How do you think Annie's success will affect her marriage to
    Frank Butler?*

Do you think it will be easy for Annie to please the crowds?

Do you think life is ever easy for an entertainer?

In 1884 the great Sitting Bull, a leader of the Native Americans,
called Annie "Little Sure Shot." Later that year Annie and Frank
went to work with Buffalo Bill's Wild West show.

40   For the next seventeen years she was the best shot in the show,
and people came from miles around to see her perform.

Frank Butler held a dime between his fingers. Annie shot it out
of his hand.

Frank Butler smoked a cigarette. Annie shot it out of his mouth.

Annie Oakley was amazingly quick. In her show, she did this

45   trick: when someone released two clay pigeons, Annie jumped over a
table, picked up a gun, and shot both targets.

Sometimes people got free tickets to go to a show. The
management punched holes in the ticket to show it was free. Annie
was so good at shooting holes in playing cards that people called a

50   card with holes punched in it an "Annie Oakley."

Annie was a wonderful rifle shot. Her assistant threw glass balls
into the air. Annie hit 943 out of 1,000. Another time she used a
shotgun for nine hours and shot 4,772 out of 5,000 glass balls.

In 1887 Annie and Frank went to Queen Victoria's Golden
Jubilee with the Wild West show. Crowds followed her through

55   London. She was so popular, and so successful, that Frank arranged
a tour of Europe. Her public life was very busy, and noisy, and bright.

What do you think Annie did when she was not performing?

Her private life was very different. She was a very religious
woman, and off-stage she lived quietly and carefully. Annie did not
have any children, but she supported orphans by giving money to

60   people who ran orphanages, or homes for orphans. In her spare
time she liked to do embroidery, and her needlework was very
beautiful.

In 1901 Annie was hurt in a terrible train wreck. Several people
died, and more than one hundred were injured. Annie fought hard

65   just to stay alive, but she was badly hurt. Her husband, Frank Butler,

stayed by her bedside. He said that he watched her light reddish hair go white within days.

It took five operations and two painful years for Annie Oakley to shoot again, but she did. However, her days of jumping over tables 70 were over. She walked more carefully than before.

During World War I, Annie Oakley and Frank Butler went around army camps, teaching and giving exhibitions. Annie was more than fifty years old, and she was still a star. But bad luck was waiting for her again.

75 In 1921 Annie was badly hurt again, this time in a car accident. She went back home to Darke County where she was born, where she died five years later. Frank Butler died twenty days after Annie and was buried beside her.

AFTER THE STORY

A. Work with a classmate, and answer these questions.

1. Did Annie Oakley surprise you? Why?

2. How accurate were your group's predictions? Where were your ideas different from those of other groups?

B. **Read the story again**. Look at the pictures. Work with a classmate, and try to guess the meaning of the words you don't know. If you can't guess, you may look in the dictionary.

C. Now answer these questions.

1. For each statement, check under **T** (true), **F** (false), or **P** (probably). If your answer is *Probably*, please explain why. We did the first one for you.

	T	F	P
1. Annie's father was very young when he died. *She was only six. He was probably very young, but he may have been in his early sixties.*			✔
2. Annie's real name was Phoebe Ann Oakley Moses.			
3. Annie loved Frank Butler very much.			
4. Annie enjoyed being an entertainer.			
5. Frank Butler was a very good shot.			

2. Scan the story, and find the lines where Annie Oakley uses a rifle to shoot glass balls. Write the line numbers here: _____–_____.

   How many glass balls did she hit? _____.

D. Look at these words, and underline the word in each row which has a different meaning. We did the first one for you.

1. famous   well known   <u>nervous</u>
2. perform   smoke   entertain
3. tickets   wreck   accident
4. arrange   hurt   injure
5. contest   manager   competition
6. gun   rifle   cigarette
7. stage   embroidery   needlework

E. Work with a classmate.

1. How does this story make you feel about Annie Oakley? Work with your partner, and make a summary of her life. Put the good things in one column and the bad things in the other.

Good Things   Bad Things

_____

_____

_____

_____

_____

_____

_____

_____

_____

_____

2. Work with your partner. Prepare an advertising poster for Annie Oakley's show. Tell people what they can expect to see.

   OR

3. Work with your partner. Write the script for a radio advertisement for Annie Oakley's show. Describe Annie, and tell people what they can expect her to do. How do people speak when they read advertisements? Try to speak like that.

F. Talk with your classmates.

1. Do your classmates play any sports or have any special skills or hobbies? Find out what another person in the class does, and write it on the chalkboard. Work with your group and classify the activities on the chalkboard as sport, hobby, or special skill. Some things will fall into two categories. For example, Annie Oakley's needlework was both a hobby and a special skill.

2. Talk to someone in the class about something they like to do. Tell the class about it. Say who the person is, what he or she does, and why you were impressed.

BEYOND THE STORY

G. Now do these activities.

1. Go to the library and try to find out more about Annie Oakley and Buffalo Bill's Wild West show.

2. Find a copy of *Annie Get Your Gun,* a musical play by Irving Berlin. The story is based on Annie Oakley's life, but it makes a lot of changes. For instance, it makes it seem as though Frank and Annie were rivals working against each other, rather than partners working together.

3. Work with a partner, and discuss Annie's relationship with her husband, Frank Butler. What may have made it difficult? Was it a good marriage? How do we know?

9

POCAHONTAS
1595(?)–1617

Pocahontas was the daughter of Powantan, a very powerful Native American chief. (People used to say Red Indian, or Indian, but it is more accurate to say Native American.) Powantan was ruler of the land where the English first made their homes in Virginia. Some of the Native Americans wanted to kill all the English people quickly, before they could take any more land.

You are going to read a story telling how Pocahontas saved the life of Captain John Smith, an Englishman captured by the Native Americans. We don't know if it really happened. We do, however, have Captain Smith's story, and this story is based on what he said.

Pocahontas was very important to Captain Smith and the other English settlers in Jamestown, because she persuaded her father to bring food to them.

POCAHONTAS SAVING THE LIFE
OF CAPTAIN JOHN SMITH
DECEMBER, 1607

MATOAKA ALS REBECCA FILIA POTENTISS : PRINC : POWHATANI IMP : VIRGINIÆ .

Ætatis suæ 21. Aᵒ 1616.

Matoaks als Rebecka daughter to the mighty Prince
Powhatan Emperour of Attanoughskomouck als virginia
converted and baptized in the Christian faith, and
wife to the worᵗ Mᵗ Joh Rolff.

Pubᵈ Aug. 10. 1793. by W. Richardson Castle Sᵗ Leicester Square.

POCAHONTAS AND CAPTAIN JOHN SMITH

BEFORE THE STORY

Talk to your classmates. Be ready to tell your teacher what other people in your group said.

1. Look at the pictures on pages 104 and 105. Then answer these questions.

    a. In the first picture, you can see Pocahontas protecting Captain Smith. Work with your partner or group, and ask each other questions about what the people in the picture are doing, how they feel, and how the picture makes you feel when you look at it.

    b. The second picture shows Pocahontas wearing English clothes. Her name is now Lady Rebecca Rolfe. Why do you think she is wearing English clothes? Where is she? Why does she have a different name? What do you think has happened? Write what your group thinks here.

    _____

    _____

    _____

    _____

    _____

2. Find Virginia on the map on page 25.

3. Show the teacher what these words mean

    excited   shiver   puzzled   intently   argue   seize

4. **Now read the story once, or listen while your teacher reads. Don't worry if you don't understand all the words when you first read a story. Just try to get the main idea.**

POCAHONTAS AND CAPTAIN JOHN SMITH

Pocahontas was the daughter of Powantan, a great chief of the native Americans. Pocahontas knew that she was her father's favorite child. Powantan loved her dearly. He talked with Pocahontas and told her many things. Pocahontas
5 listened closely and was quick to learn. She knew that Powantan was worried because the English were in his land.

It was the year 1608, and there were a few English settlers in Virginia. Powantan was not sure what to do.

"I wish I knew what the English plan to do," Powantan told his
10 daughter. "I don't want them here. I wish they'd go away."

"Many English settlers died last winter," Pocahontas said.

"That's true," Powantan said. "But there are some left. What if they want to stay here? They take our land, and they trap the animals."

15 "Perhaps they'll get in their boat and go back across the sea," Pocahontas said.

Powantan kept on worrying. "I don't like it at all," he said. "It's going to be hard to make them leave. It seems cruel to chase the English away, but many of our people are angry. They want to kill
20 them, or send them back where they came from. I'm not sure . . ."

Just then a messenger ran toward Powantan.

"We've caught one of the English thieves," he said.

Powantan said, "Call a meeting of the people."

What do you think will happen to the Englishman?

Pocahontas watched the people prepare for the meeting. Her
25 father, Powantan, sat higher than the rest. He looked worried. Pocahontas shivered. Everyone was waiting, and they were speaking quietly. Then they stopped talking, and turned to watch the warriors bring the Englishman before Powantan.

The crowd made a great roaring sound, like an angry wind.
30 Everyone looked at the pioneer.

Powantan pointed, and Captain Smith came to stand in front of him. Then Powantan waved his hand, and the Queen of Appamatuck came from the crowd. She carried a bowl of water and held it for Captain Smith to wash his hands.

35   Captain Smith did not know what to do. He looked puzzled and afraid. The queen held the bowl out to him again, and he dipped his hands in it. The crowd watched intently, waiting for something . . .

Another woman came from the crowd and handed Captain Smith a bunch of feathers. He dried his hands on them.

40   Powantan nodded, and the people sighed again. Servants came with an enormous meal. There was every sort of food: corn, venison, fish, yams—all spread for a great feast.

Pocahontas watched as everybody ate. Captain Smith still looked afraid, but he ate well. Pocahontas knew that all the people in the

45   English settlement were hungry. They did not know how to grow food.

The feast went on and on. After a long time, when everybody's stomach was full, Powantan called the most important people in the room. He called the men who fought the best, his bravest warriors,

50   and the wise old people of the tribe.

Pocahontas watched while they talked. It went on for a long time. As they argued, the people looked at Captain Smith. They looked angry. She heard someone say, "If we let them stay, we'll all be hungry." Another voice said, "They'll die of starvation. They don't know how to grow food properly. They don't even know what to eat."

55   All the voices grew louder and angrier.

At last they stopped talking. Everyone moved back from the center of the room. Strong men dragged two great stones and placed them in front of Powantan.

Then the strongest men seized Captain Smith, and they threw

60   him onto the stones. He lay still. The warriors gathered around and lifted their clubs in the air.

Pocahontas slipped out of the crowd and ran through the hall. She saw her father's surprised face and the angry faces of her people. She saw the raised clubs, and she threw herself across

65   Captain Smith's body. Her head protected his. The cruel clubs had to hit her first.

Powantan ordered the warriors back.

"What are you doing, my child?" he asked sternly.

Pocahontas looked up. "Let him live," she said simply, "Or club

70   me to death. I will not let go."

Powantan thought for a while. Then he said, "It will be as you say. Get up, my child."

Powantan spoke to his people. "We will let him live," he said. Then he laughed. "We will give him work to do. He will make beads and bells for my daughter Pocahontas. If he does that well, he may make hatchets for our men."

75

The crowd laughed at the idea of a fighting man making toys and hatchets.

How do you think Captain Smith will like making beads and bells and hatchets?

Why do you think Powantan chose this punishment?

So Pocahontas saved Captain John Smith. We do not know if this is a true story. However, many people in the United States know about Pocahontas and Captain Smith, mainly because Captain Smith wrote an account in his *Generall Historie*, printed in London in 1624.

80

Later, Captain Smith went home to Jamestown. Powantan showed the settlers how to grind corn, and they lived better than before.

Pocahontas made changes all her short life. She became a Christian in 1613, and in 1614 she married John Rolfe, an English tobacco planter. Powantan agreed to the marriage, and there was peace between the settlers and the Native Americans for the next eight years.

85

In 1615 Pocahontas bore a baby boy, Thomas. In 1616 she went to England, and the people she met loved her. Pocahontas took the Christian name of Rebecca. John Rolfe was now Sir John Rolfe, so Pocahontas was called Lady Rebecca Rolfe in England.

90

Pocahontas died in 1617 while preparing to return to Virginia. She is buried at Gravesend near London, where you can see a statue in her honor.

95

AFTER THE STORY

A. Work with a classmate, and answer these questions.

1. Why didn't the people kill Captain Smith?

2. How accurate were your group's predictions?

B. Read the story again. Look at the pictures. Work with a classmate, and try to guess the meaning of the words you don't know. If you can't guess, you may look in the dictionary.

C. Match the beginning of the sentence with the end. We did the first one for you.

1. Pocahontas was   a. an Englishman named John Rolfe.

2. Powantan was worried   b. she was preparing to return.

3. Powantan wanted the settlers   c. named Thomas.

4. Pocahontas saved Captain Smith   d. the daughter of Powantan.

5. Later she married   e. to go away.

6. They had a baby boy   f. from being clubbed to death.

7. Pocahontas died in England while   g. by the English settlers.

D. Match the words with their meanings. We did the first one for you.

1. favorite   a. things you can ring

2. trap   b. a huge meal

3. magnificent   c. best loved

4. enormous   d. a heavy weapon

5. feast   e. small balls with holes in the middle

6. drag   f. catch

7. club   g. to pull without lifting off the ground

8. beads   h. great, grand, awe-inspiring

9. bells   i. extremely big

E. Pretend you are Pocahontas. Work with a classmate, and tell what happened in your life. Start from when the English settlers arrived. Tell about what Powantan said and felt, and tell about Captain Smith and John Rolfe.

F. Talk about the story.

1. Read from lines 29 to 50 on pages 107 to 108. It begins, "The crowd made a great roaring sound, like an angry wind." Talk with your classmates about how Captain Smith felt and about what he did. Then write a paragraph about him. Be ready to share your paragraph with the rest of the class, perhaps by putting it on the chalkboard. Did all the groups agree?

2. Did Pocahontas save Captain Smith? Captain Smith published his story in London after Pocahontas died. Who could check the story for facts? Do you think we will ever find out? Why would Smith lie? Write the opinions of different members of your group.

Name	Did Pocahontas save Captain Smith? (Write *Yes* or *No*)	Reason for the answer

BEYOND THE STORY

G. Now do these activities.

1. Go to the library and find out more about Jamestown. Why did the English go there? What happened to the settlement during Pocahontas's lifetime?

2. On line 53 on page 108, someone says, "They'll die of starvation. They don't know how to grow food properly. They don't even know what to eat." Ask people in your family about growing and preparing food. Is it done differently in different places? Be ready to share with the class what you learn.

3. How do you think Pocahontas felt while she lived in England? Was it fun for her? Have you ever been in a strange new place? How did you feel? Tell your classmates or write about it.

Photo and Illustration Credits

page 2   John Henry
Illustration by Frank Cyrsky.

page 14   George Washington
Courtesy of the Library of Congress. The picture was painted by G. G. White, engraved by John G. McRae, and published by Mr. McRae at 100 Liberty Street, New York City. It was entered according to Act of Congress in 1867 in the Clerk's Office of the U.S. District Court for the Southern District of New York.

page 24   Johnny Appleseed
Courtesy of the Oberlin College Library. This picture is the earliest known drawing of Johnny Appleseed. It was supposedly drawn in the 1850s by an Oberlin College student who knew him.

page 34   Paul Bunyan
Illustration by Frank Cyrsky.

page 44   logjam
Courtesy of U.S. Forest Service.

page 48   Casey Jones
Courtesy of Illinois Central Railroad.

page 48   Engine 382
Courtesy of Illinois Central Railroad. This is the engine that Casey Jones was driving when he died.

page 60   Davy Crockett addressing crowd
Courtesy of the Tennessee State Museum.

page 61   Davy Crockett and Job Snelling
Illustration by Frank Cyrsky

page 72   Davy Crockett and Peg-Leg Huntsman
Illustration by Frank Cyrsky

pages 80 and 81   Calamity Jane
    Courtesy of the Buffalo Bill Historical Center, Cody, Wyoming.

pages 93 and 94   Annie Oakley
    Courtesy of the Buffalo Bill Historical Center, Cody, Wyoming.

page 104   Pocahontas and Captain John Smith
    Courtesy of the Continental Insurance Company.

page 105   Pocahontas (portrait)
    Courtesy of the Fogg Art Museum, Harvard University.